MOTIVATING AND INSPIRING TEACHERS

THE EDUCATIONAL LEADER'S GUIDE
FOR BUILDING STAFF MORALE

Todd Whitaker
Beth Whitaker
Dale Lumpa

EYE ON EDUCATION
6 Depot Way West, Suite 106
Larchmont, N.Y. 10538

Library of Congress Cataloging-in-Publication Data

Whitaker, Todd, 1959-
    Motivating and inspiring teachers : the educational leader's guide for building staff
morale / by Todd Whitaker, Beth Whitaker, and Dale Lumpa.
        p. cm.
    Includes bibliographical references (p.).
    ISBN 1-883001-99-4
    1. Teacher morale. 2. Motivation in education. 3. School environment. 4. School
management and organization. I. Whitaker, Beth, 1960- II. Lumpa, Dale, 1961- III.
Title.

LB2840 .W45 2000
371.2'01--dc21

                                                                        00-02491

 PRINTED IN CANADA

Production services provided by:
Bookwrights
1211 Courtland Drive
Raleigh, NC 27604

ABOUT THE AUTHORS

Dr. Todd Whitaker is an Associate Professor of Educational Leadership at Indiana State University in Terre Haute, Indiana. Prior to coming to Indiana, he was a middle and high school principal for eight years in Missouri. His previous book, *Dealing with Difficult Teachers*, is currently in its fourth printing. His next work is entitled *Dealing with Difficult Parents (and with Parents in Difficult Situations)*.

Todd is a highly sought-after speaker for teachers and principals. He has made hundreds of presentations, including keynote addresses at state conferences, school district opening sessions, and numerous national presentations.

Dr. Beth Whitaker is an Assistant Professor of Elementary and Early Childhood Education at Indiana State University in Terre Haute, Indiana. Beth was principal at Thorpe J. Gordon Elementary School in Jefferson City, Missouri, which received the National Blue Ribbon Award for School Excellence.

Dr. Whitaker has been published in the areas of school climate, principal leadership, and staff motivation and morale. She also works with many principals, teachers, and schools in the areas of curriculum development, classroom management, writing, and reading. Todd and Beth are co-editors of *Contemporary Education*, an international peer-reviewed journal.

Dr. Dale Lumpa is a principal at Charles Hay Elementary School in Englewood, Colorado. He has been an administrator at the elementary and middle school levels for 12 years, including principalships in school districts in Missouri and Colorado.

Dr. Lumpa has presented at state and national conferences on effective discipline and positive strategies for educational leaders. He is active in the Colorado Principals' Center, serving on the board of directors. He is an adjunct professor for the University of Phoenix in the Denver area.

PREFACE

Our interest in writing this book comes from our experiences as teachers, as principals, and working with school faculties across the country. Teaching is one of the most important professions there is. Being able to approach work every day in a positive state of mind is critical to being successful with the students we work with. All educators entered the profession with the idea of positively impacting young people. However, completing paperwork, resolving conflicts, and maintaining the high level of energy needed each day can take their toll on this positive focus.

As teachers we realized that we must meet this challenge if we are to be effective. If we lose our patience, behave unprofessionally, or react inappropriately, then we have not maintained the level of performance that is needed in order to be effective in the classroom. Additionally, if we are rude or sarcastic to others, they are likely to react to us in that same fashion. Then, we are likely to escalate this cycle with someone else. This bad day then becomes a *terrible* day and our state of mind is even more negative. And, more importantly, we have affected the students in a manner that was the opposite of our belief system. Thus, as educators our personal morale must consistently be at a high level.

When we became principals, the realization that the effectiveness of our staff will determine the effectiveness of our schools caused us to see the need for a highly motivated, positive group of adults working with students each day. When teachers are in a bad mood, they may react inappropriately to students. When this occurs, the students snap back or take out their aggressions on other faculty members or on their peers. As this gets compounded, eventually this cycle winds its way back to the principal. So in addition to the benefit to the students, we have a selfish incentive to keep the focus positive in the school.

In working with schools we have discovered that one of the greatest needs of faculty and staff is a more positive morale. This is true in every school. No matter what the morale level is, educators consistently describe one of their top needs as "having higher morale." Climate surveys, assessments of professional development needs, and informal discussions consistently indicate the desire for a higher level of morale.

All of us wish that we could have a positive outlook at work every day. Everyone wants to be enthusiastic about what they do. Educators know that it is their obligation as professionals to approach each day in a "thank God it's Monday" frame of mind! This book is a guide to help educational leaders maintain their own positive focus each day. Even more importantly, it provides specific guidance for educational leaders to help increase the morale of their entire staff.

DEDICATION

This book is dedicated to Dale's wife and parents, Kay Lumpa and Bill and Janet Lumpa, and to Beth's and Todd's parents, Tapley and Charlene McCune and Curtis and Avis Whitaker. It is also dedicated to our children, Mariah and Jillian Lumpa and Katherine, Madeline, and Harrison Whitaker. Every day we work to build your morale and every day you build ours. We love you.

Todd's father, J. Curtis Whitaker, passed away during the writing of this book. He was a true teller of stories and tales aimed at making people laugh and smile. We dedicate any laughter or happiness that comes from this book to him.

INTRODUCTION

Our core belief is that education is the single most important profession. We feel that it is essential that all educators approach their work in a positive and enthusiastic frame of mind every day. There is no room for cynics in education. We truly do have to believe in what we do in order to be effective.

Interestingly, because we believe high staff morale is so critical, and because it applies to every school, we assumed that there were many books on building staff morale for educators. Surprisingly, such books are almost nonexistent. When I ask educators why they believe this to be so, the most common answer is, "having high staff morale is critical, but few people know *how* to enhance it." So, with that challenge in mind, we decided to develop a book for educational leaders and educators of all types. We hope the book can help remind us of the importance of positive staff morale, provide guidance for increasing the morale of those around us, and also—maybe most importantly—increase our own morale.

I like to tell a story when I speak to educational groups. Let me share it with you. Picture yourself in an auditorium full of teachers…

"I truly believe that education is the most important profession. I also believe that it is the profession with the highest expectations. I believe that the only acceptable standard for education is the standard of greatness. Now, this greatness standard may sound ridiculously high, but we have a room full of educational experts here, so let's take a quiz.

"How many of you have children? How many of you want your children to go to *okay* schools with *fairly good* teachers?"

Typically, two or three hands go up out of a hundred.

"I see a couple of hands raised. I am assuming that those hands went up because your children go to worse schools than that and have teachers less effective than 'fairly good.'

"Okay, how many of you want your children to go to great schools with outstanding teachers?"

Every hand in the room is raised.

"Well, the challenge we all face is that the families of every single young person who walks through our classroom doors each day have these same high expectations. And the reason their expectations are so high is because what we do is so important. They have turned over their most prized possessions to us and they want the best for them."

The challenge for us as educators is to remember that we have chosen the most important profession, and it is essential that we remind ourselves of this every day. The additional challenge for educational leaders is to help those we work with feel this level of importance each day. In education, we cannot afford to have a bad day—simply because the students we work with never deserve to have a bad day because of us.

This book is designed to help educational leaders consistently and continually build and cultivate a positive morale throughout their faculty and staff. The approaches in this book are very straightforward and can be applied in every educational setting immediately. Though many of the examples for the concepts are given from the point of view of the principal, educational leaders of all types, and any educator, can apply them in their own setting. Either a superintendent or a department chair can utilize a Friday Focus memo. Developing a vision is just as important for a middle school team leader as it is for a building-level leader. Modeling appropriate ways to interact with students is equally applicable to a grade-level leader and to a principal. Informal teacher leaders can also practice the approaches described in this book. All educators need to make sure that they take care of their own morale. When it comes to the link between building morale and educational leadership, the more the merrier. If these practices can be implemented district-wide, school-wide, and throughout the various levels of the school, the entire faculty and staff will be the better for it. And, as a result, so will the students.

The challenge for educational leaders is to make sure that we approach every day and each situation with a positive frame of mind. The ability to sustain this perspective is critical if we are to infuse this attitude throughout our schools. Also essential is the ability to apply this approach in a multitude of situations.

Each individual idea presented in this book is understandable and simple. Like most things of value, though, they are simple—but not easy. The easy things we have already accomplished.

TABLE OF CONTENTS

PART 1

THE ROLE OF THE LEADER

1

WHY IT ALL WORKS

As soon as you walk into a school, any school, you can sense the level of excitement and energy, or lack thereof, in the building. The same is true when you venture into a classroom or hallway of a school. What is it that differentiates the places that are exciting to work from those that lack the energy and excitement essential to a high-functioning school? One factor is the morale and motivation of those who work at the school. How can we get *our* schools to be like the "high-excitement" educational centers? Once that spark of excitement is ignited, are there things we can do to build on this momentum? How can we maintain the energy of the first day of school all year long?

Whether your school is one that consistently has a high level of excitement or one where by the end of the first week someone writes the number of days until Christmas vacation on the chalkboard in the teachers' lounge, there are several things that affect your school. One of the struggles we had in writing this book involved determining what to include in Chapter 1.

As principals, we often scoffed at theories—if we thought any inservice or article was even going to mention the word, we would readily opt out. This instinct also rang true when we were writing the book. We couldn't wait to get to what the heart of being a principal was all about. However, we also thought it was important to lay a brief foundation of why the dynamics of schools are as they are. What is it that causes some schools to be dynamic and others to be duds? We felt that we had to include some background information in Chapter 1 that would help each of us understand where schools are and how they got there. Thus, in this chapter we are laying out five theories that we feel are essential in developing an understanding of dynamics and morale. If that "practitioner urge" gets to be too strong, feel free to skip immediately to Chapter 2 and dive in when you are ready. If you would like to get your toes wet first, however, as you read, think about the people you work with and how they fit into these models.

The general approaches outlined in these theories can provide a rich foundation for understanding why the specifics from the rest of the book actually will work to build a dynamic environment in your school. You may have heard of some of these ideas, like Maslow's hierarchy of needs (1970) and Herzberg's motivational-hygiene theory (Herzberg, Mausner, and Snyderman 1993). Others, like the Group Norm (Mayo 1933) or Comparison Other (Lunenburg and Ornstein 1996) may not be so familiar. However, one thing that is critical in all settings is the role of the leader(s).

In a school, the obvious formal leader is the principal. Additionally, there may be many informal leaders, as well as others with positional power: department chairs, team leaders, grade-level leaders, and so on. Each of these people can play a significant role in the morale of those around them. Let's apply a few theories to an understanding of how morale can be affected in a school.

MASLOW'S HIERARCHY OF NEEDS

Maslow's theory of the hierarchy of needs is a widely used study of motivation in organizations, including schools. According to Lunenburg and Ornstein (1996), Maslow identified five basic groups of human needs that emerge in a specific sequence or pattern—that is, in a hierarchy of importance. Once one need is satisfied, another emerges and demands satisfaction, and so on through the hierarchy. These five levels of need, which represent the order of importance to the individual, are physiological, safety and security, social, esteem, and self-actualization (p. 89).

These needs, arranged from lowest level to highest level, are as follows:

1. **Physiological needs** include the basics of food, water, sleep, oxygen, and the like.
2. **Safety and security needs** include the need for physical safety, avoidance of anxiety, order, structure, and job and financial security.
3. **Social needs** include the need for belonging to groups, friendship, and acceptance by others.
4. **Esteem needs** include the need for self-respect, appreciation, and recognition from others.
5. **Self-actualization needs** include the desire for maximizing your own potential, autonomy, and creativity.

The reason that these are related to morale is that if the low-level physiological, safety, and social needs are not satisfied, then the individual is not likely to have a positive morale. Only when more basic needs are met can people shift their emphasis to fulfilling their esteem and self-actualization needs. This motivation for recognition, self-respect, and maximizing your potential is a critical part of being motivated.

Understanding where everyone is on the hierarchy can help a leader give people what they need in order to be more motivated in the workplace. A person can have certain needs met in one circumstance but not in another. A recent example involves all of the tragedies related to violence in schools across the country. Teachers who previously had little concern for their safety at work may have become much more insecure about their safety in their school. However, this may not have resulted in a diminished level of comfort at home, in social circumstances, at church, or in other situations.

Educational leaders, then, must realize that the teachers and staff members of their organizations must have their safety needs met before they can establish or reestablish a higher morale level. However, it is also important to be aware that to a large degree, *these needs are from the perspective of the beholder*. They are not from the perspective of the leader. Let's take an example using safety and security. It is not enough for staff members just to *be* safe; they must also *feel* safe. If a teacher feels threatened by a student in class, the principal must not only be sure that the student will do no harm, but also help the teacher to feel safe. The recent highly publicized violent incidents in school did not necessarily change the safety of other schools; however, it greatly impacted the way parents, students, and staff members feel about the safety of their schools. These parents, students, and staff moved down to a basic need level and they need satisfaction that these concerns will be addressed before they can move back up the hierarchy.

As educational leaders work to enhance morale in their organizations, one of the aspects of Maslow's hierarchy that may come into play more than any other is the social needs of teachers. As principals wonder why teachers often sit in the teachers' lounge and gripe, or why so many meetings can turn into whine sessions, one explanation may be the social needs of people. The concept of "fitting in" is critical. I may not inherently be a negative person, but if that dynamic is established in the teachers' lunchroom, lounge, or workroom, then behaving like everyone else can be part of belonging. Understanding this influence can be very helpful when deciding room location, grade level, or planning time for staff members. Also, taking advantage of opportunities to build morale by having as many staff as possible associate with positive staff can be an easy way to have this productive attitude infiltrate the school.

People of all ages are similar. Think about the new student in a school who does not know anyone. When he first arrives he does not have a peer group. If the new student does not feel that he fits in at school, which group will always take the student in? It will not be the popular students or the high achievers. The group of more negative students always has room for one more. The same is true of a school staff. Rather than hoping a new teacher does not join a negative group at the staff meeting or in the lounge, make an effort to link the new teacher with productive members. This is often doubly important if gender, department, grade level, or some other natural pull is involved. Everyone wants to fit in; this can be a crucial element in our personal morale.

THE IMPORTANCE OF TRUST

We can never lose sight of the value of the feelings of others and their impact on morale. When a teacher refers a student to the office for discipline, the teacher does not just want to *be* supported, but wants to *feel* supported. If the principal who handles the discipline does not communicate effectively with the teacher what is done in support, the teacher still feels unsupported regardless of what the administrative action was. However, if the administrator can make the teacher feel supported, then the specific disciplinary action becomes much less relevant.

Similarly, when people are asked to list characteristics of an effective leader, one that often comes up is a good listener. However, I would argue that we want more than that. We do not just want a good listener; we want someone who makes us feel listened to.

I would bet that many of you have the ability to multi-task very effectively. In other words, you can type on your computer while talking on the phone, or read the newspaper while watching television. However, what happens in our leadership role is that if people we work with do not feel we are a good listener, it probably does not matter whether we are or not. If someone comes to talk to you and you continue to look at the computer screen during the visit, that person will feel that you did not listen—whether you did or not. Thus, regardless of your action or response, their level of regard for you personally, their trust, is likely to diminish. However, if you look them in the eye and even just pretend to actively listen, their personal regard for you is much more likely to be positive.

It is essential that these feelings of trust continue to rise between leaders and those they work with. If these do not get established, then the leader will continually be second-guessed by others. The willingness to respond in a positive manner to ideas, suggestions, or directives from a leader was described by Chester Barnard (1938) as the "zone of indifference." Barnard believed that all workers have a zone of indifference in which they are willing to do what their supervisor says without questioning the rationale for the decision. He also believed that different workers have different zones of indifference. In other words, a trusting worker might have a very large zone of indifference, whereas a cynical worker may have a very small zone of indifference, or even none at all (Figure 1).

The larger the zone of indifference employees have, the more smoothly a leader's decisions can be implemented and supported. To a leader, having workers with large zones of indifference can be very appealing. The question, of course, is "How can we influence this zone of indifference?"

The essential link between leadership and the size of others' zones of indifference is the level of trust that the leader has established. The higher the level of trust someone has, the larger the zone of indifference.

FIGURE 1

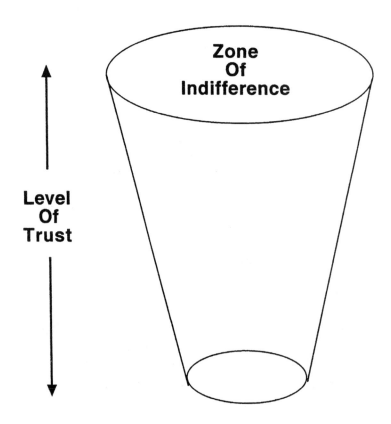

The concept is that if people trust someone, they tend to do less second-guessing of their everyday decisions. However, when a leader has not established trust, then everyone in the organization continually questions, at least internally, every decision made. Thus, they stay at a lower point on their level of morale.

If we, as leaders, find ourselves in a situation where we are consistently being second-guessed over the most minor decisions, the solution may not be to attempt to put more energy into decision making. We may be better served by focusing on increasing the level of trust we have with those in their organization.

Again, the level of trust may be based as much on perception as reality. Though people's trust of us may be based substantially on perceptions, the resulting impact on our ability to lead effectively is very much based in reality. And, as in many circumstances, when there is a *perceived* lack of leadership, everyone tries to fill the void. The school board starts to micromanage, the teacher organization begins to question everything, and morale is greatly diminished. Understanding this link between trust and indifference is essential for a leader. If we cannot establish this bond, every decision we make will be much more likely to be put under a microscope by all of the Monday-morning quarterbacks in our organization. Being aware of the effect of a lack of trust can help us place more emphasis on continually working to enhance these relations.

Let's take a look at a common example. I worked in a school district where the superintendent was not viewed as an effective leader. This superintendent, like many in the Midwest, faces a familiar situation during the winter: the decision must be made whether to cancel school when there is inclement weather. In the district where I was, the superintendent with the perceived lack of leadership was constantly second-guessed. This was true even if the decision was a good one! If we had a significant snowstorm and school was canceled, the only thing you heard was "We could have had school," or "It wasn't bad at all." If there was a wintry forecast that did not materialize into bad weather and we went ahead and had school, many people would say that we should have canceled, because "It could have turned really bad outside."

When this superintendent retired, we were fortunate to have a dynamic leader who immediately built up trusting relations with all constituents. Amazingly, even when he made *incorrect* decisions he was supported. If there was a threatening forecast and school was canceled yet the bad weather never arrived, I would hear those same previous critics say, "Better safe than sorry." If we had school and then there was a terrible storm, the response was "Hindsight is 20–20." Developing a high level of trust between leader and staff members is essential in order to have positive morale in an organization.

HERZBERG'S MOTIVATION-HYGIENE THEORY

One of the challenges of an educational leader regarding staff morale is the lack of control that most leaders have involving tangible benefits such as pay, benefits, and the like. A principal has little influence on teacher pay and a department chair often has no ability to affect the salaries of the members of the department. Thus, the least effective person may be the highest paid. This lack of control may make us feel that we cannot positively affect the morale of others because we cannot provide monetary reinforcements. However, Frederick Herzberg provided a different perspective regarding what motivates people (Herzberg, Mausner, and Snyderman 1993). Herzberg developed a two-factor theory which consists of hygiene factors, or dissatisfiers, and motivational factors, or satisfiers.

The hygiene factors, or dissatisfiers, consist of traditional incentives like salary, benefits, and vacations. They are referred to as dissatisfiers because if they do not seem adequate it can be demotivating for people, yet if there is a minimal satisfactory level achieved, they seldom provide a long-term incentive.

Think about your own work situation. If your salary is at least at an adequate level, how much harder would you work next year if your salary were going to be doubled? Maybe a little bit more the first day, week, or even month, but then you would settle into your previous level of performance. If you question this, then ask yourself: If it were doubled again the following year, how much harder would you work? What if it were doubled again? Obviously, while this salary increase would be nice, it would not likely result in an increased motivation and productivity level.

Herzberg explains that motivational factors are recognition, achievement, responsibility, and things of a more intrinsic nature. Praise, acknowledgement, and positive reinforcement fit into this category. Herzberg's theory is an important one for educational leaders because the essential items such as complimenting someone, allowing someone autonomy in their duties, and providing recognition are things that school leaders do have control over. If money and benefits were the only incentives, then principals, department chairs, and grade-level leaders would not have much to go on. Understanding that we *can* provide the interpersonal things that most affect morale is very reinforcing to the educational leader.

Understanding this dynamic is a basis for this book. It is essential that leaders recognize that they have a tremendous influence on others in their organization. Herzberg's theory is very empowering for those who use these motivational factors. As leaders, we should be encouraged that the things that have the greatest impact on positively influencing others are the things that we have the most ability to control. This provides a great opportunity *and* a great responsibility.

COMPARISON OTHER

The concept of Comparison Other (Lunenburg and Ornstein 1996) is important in understanding how to affect staff morale positively. Have you ever worked with someone who you felt did much less work than you and yet was paid the same or even more? How did this make you feel? Have you ever had a supervisor compliment a coworker that you felt did not deserve it, when you have not received similar praise for your efforts? How did you feel? Did this motivate you to work harder, or did it frustrate and demoralize you? Did it seem unfair? This frustration and the effort to avoid similar situations is at the heart of the theory of Comparison Other.

The concept of Comparison Other is related to the concept of fairness, except it goes one step further. This theory says that we not only look at others to determine if the "rewards" we get are adequate, but also examine the level of work they do to see if it too is equitable. We then compare the ratio of our outcomes and inputs to coworkers' outcomes and inputs. Another way to examine the same concept is to compare the ratio of contributions/efforts to rewards/recognition for ourselves and our Comparison Other (Figure 2).

If we feel that our ratio of contributions to rewards is higher than someone else's, then our morale is negatively affected. There are only two ways to achieve balance: to lower the level of contributions or efforts we make, or to increase our level of rewards and recognition.

It is essential that leaders at all levels recognize this concept of Comparison Other. If we do not, then the effort level of our highest achievers is likely to be diminished. And, as we will discover in the next chapter, the motivation level of our best employees, our superstars, is critical to the morale of the entire school.

Educational leaders may find the concept of Comparison Other very discouraging. We may feel that because we have little or no impact on salary, benefits, or other tangibles, we cannot

---

FIGURE 2

Outcomes (employee)		**Outcomes (comparison others)**
───────	**versus**	───────────
Inputs (employee)		**Inputs (comparison others)**

Contributions/Efforts (employee)		**Contributions/Efforts (comparison others)**
───────	**versus**	───────────
Rewards/Recognitions (employee)		**Rewards/Recognitions (comparison others)**

impact the level of rewards and recognition that our most effective teachers and staff receive. This lack of salary influence may be true to some degree with all professions, but it is even more so in education. The salaries of educators are usually based on a salary schedule that has little or nothing to do with effectiveness. So how can we resolve a seeming conflict between a very effective teacher who makes the same as, or less than, a less effective (and less hardworking) peer?

Overcoming this inequity has everything to do with leadership. As leaders, what we have to do is increase the level of outcomes based on the effectiveness of employees. We must look for intangible ways to increase the level of rewards and recognition that our most effective employees receive. Instead of feeling limited because of our lack of influence on salary, principals and other educational leaders must focus on other types of rewards and recognition. In other words, we must positively reinforce the efforts of people based on efforts and success. Leave notes, give praise, provide autonomy, to boost the morale of high achievers. And, if the opportunity ever arises, allow them additional professional development opportunities, budget monies, and so on, as appropriate. We have to make every effort to ensure that people who work harder (inputs) feel that they receive more reinforcement for their efforts (outputs). It is essential that we accomplish this in order to continue to have a high effort level with our most productive staff members. We will specifically address effective ways to do this in upcoming chapters.

GROUP NORM

The Hawthorne studies, conducted by Elton Mayo and his associates between 1927 and 1933, are classic experiments regarding the effectiveness of workers. These are referred to as the Hawthorne studies because they were conducted at the Hawthorne Plant of Western Electric (Mayo 1933).

The term Hawthorne Effect resulted from an experiment in relay assembly test rooms regarding the impact of lighting on productivity. There were two rooms of female workers who were performing the same tasks. One group, which was designated as the control group, had no changes in its lighting. The other group, which was the experimental group, had its lighting and other environmental factors altered. Interestingly, regardless of the changes in the environmental factors, *both* groups had increases in productivity. The researchers concluded that the reason was not the lighting, but the *attention* paid to the workers. This was the beginning of the study of human relations and its impact on productivity and morale.

A second experiment involved a bank wiring observation room in which a group of nine men were paid on a piecework incentive basis. The more they did, the more money they received. The researchers found some very surprising results. The group established an informal acceptance level of work. Most of the workers ignored the incentive system and voluntarily conformed to the group's standard level of acceptance. This level is referred to as the Group Norm. The deviants, those who did not conform, were disciplined by the group to bring their output in line with the others. The good news was that the under-producers, or "chiselers," were pressured into increasing their productivity. The bad news was that the overachievers, or "rate busters," were pressured and sometimes even threatened into conforming with the rest of the group by decreasing their productivity.

Not only does this reinforce the concept of Maslow's social need, but also it has implications for educational leaders. As a leader attempts to have people increase their efforts, the group may attempt to keep high achievers from succeeding. Successfully walking this fine line is essential. When we hire new people, usually our goal is to make our organization more like the new people than it is to make the new people more like our organization. The concept of the Group Norm works against this success. Chapter 15 explains the importance of new people to an organization and describes how to successfully support the efforts of new members, and others, who are high achievers.

This chapter has highlighted a few of the theories that apply to education. We hope these will provide a basis for understanding **why** the morale is where it is in your organization. The remainder of the book will focus on **how** educational leaders can positively impact the morale of those in their organization to have a dynamic and motivated staff, **what** you can do as leader, and **who** are the people you most need to focus on in your efforts.

2

UNDERSTANDING STAFF DYNAMICS

When we think about improving the morale of a school, our instinct may be to focus on improving the morale of our most disgruntled staff. After all, the most positive people are likely to have a "pretty good" attitude already. Thus, the temptation may be to focus on the morale of our most negative staff members.

Well, as a leader, you need to start somewhere, but our perspective is that you need to start with your *most effective* people— your *superstars*. This is true regardless of their current morale level. Generally, the most effective people have a fairly good attitude toward work or else they would not be so effective. However, once we realize and accept the impact these key people have on the rest of the faculty, it is easier to understand why they are so important.

Think of it in terms of the Group Norm. We have to maintain the level of enthusiasm of the high-achieving "rate busters," or else they will fall back in line with the others. This was a positive effect when the outliers were below the norm, but very negative with overachievers. We have to continually nurture the more positive people first, before we can shift our attention to the majority. Let us provide some terminology to help understand the dynamics of our staff.

INFORMAL TEACHER LEADERS

We often think of a school as a "peer-pressure factory" for students. The same thing is true for the teachers. Often, what a few key people do and say sets the tone for the building. The influence of informal relations on a faculty cannot be overstated. Workroom discussions, team teacher talks, parking lot chats, and casual hallway conversations often have very powerful effects on the position that teachers take on an issue. They also help shape the philosophical beliefs of all faculty members.

Teacher leadership is an area that may be the most important to the change/improvement process of a school, yet it is often one of the least analyzed and discussed among educational leaders. One of the reasons for this may be that educators feel their staff is composed of unique personalities. They may believe that because of differences between the personality makeup of various faculties, there is not a common pattern of informal teacher leadership. Yet in a study of effective administrators, Whitaker and Valentine (1993) determined that effective principals identify key teacher leaders and involve them in the decision-making progress. They also use the teacher leaders in an informal manner to help the school progress with new and improved programs and curriculum.

MORE EFFECTIVE AND LESS EFFECTIVE PRINCIPALS

Whitaker (1997) identified middle schools in which principals were either one standard deviation above or one deviation below the group norm on the Audit of Principal Effectiveness—a nationally normed assessment of principals' skills. Four schools from each group were then identified based on school climate, as measured by NASSP's Comprehensive Assessment of School Environments (CASE) instrument and the level of implementation of key middle-level characteristics. In on-site visits and interviews with the principals and groups of teachers, Whitaker then studied participatory management at the more effective and less effective schools. One of the major differences between the two groups of schools was the identification and subsequent use of teacher leaders at the more effective schools and the lack thereof at the less effective schools.

Effective principals consistently were able to identify the informal teacher leaders in their buildings. They consistently indicated, and the teachers in their schools confirmed, that teacher input, direction, and suggestions for the school were sought out and consistently used. The principals also indicated that they used these informal teacher leaders for many purposes. In addition to asking their opinions before making decisions, they would have these teacher leaders carry out functions in many ways. Besides the more traditional formal procedures, such as presenting at faculty meetings and department meetings, the principals would have these teachers carry an informal message back to the workrooms, to their coworkers, and to peers within their department.

There is no question that the relationship between an effective instructional leader, i.e., the principal, and an effective school is a significant one. Yet one of the essential skills that the principal must have is the ability to identify key teacher leaders and use these individuals to assist with the change process of their schools. The level of trust that peers hold for each other makes change in this fashion much smoother and much stronger than a top-down approach.

One of the most glaring weakness of the less effective principals in the study was an inability to recognize and identify informal teacher leaders on their faculties. Because they did not rely on the informal structure of their organization, they did not have success leading their school in a positive direction. The ability to identify and benefit from these important staff members is a key to being an effective building administrator (Whitaker 1995).

A principal must also be aware of the perceptions of the teachers as to how they are involved in decision making in the school. Another key aspect of the study of more effective and less effective middle-level principals (Whitaker and Valentine 1993) was that "in effective schools, teachers and principals share the same perspectives of how much input teachers have in decision-making within their schools" (p. 22). Thus, it is critical that educational leaders consistently gather feedback as to the perceptions of their staff's view of their involvement.

Recognizing the informal leaders on a faculty may not be a

simple task. Strength of personality, outspokenness, and being friendly may be possible indicators, but there are other descriptors that can help with the identification process. The most important element is to recognize the educators in a building who are the most respected by their peers. Often, the most effective teachers are also the informal leaders among faculty. Understanding the differences among faculty members is an essential component of being an effective leader.

THREE KINDS OF TEACHERS

A perspective on understanding the different types of teachers is offered by Dr. Al Burr (1993), a former high school principal in the St. Louis area. He believes that there are three kinds of teachers in a school: **superstars, backbones,** and **mediocres.**

We feel that this is true not only in schools, but in every profession. We would guess that managers of WalMart stores could identify three kinds of clerks and that hospital administrators could identify three kinds of nurses.

In applying this to schools, Burr explained that the way to determine the category of each teacher is fairly simple. A **superstar** is that rare teacher who represents the top three to ten percent of teachers in a school. Many schools may have only one or two people who fall into this category. A few outstanding schools may have eight to ten. They are often the students' favorite teachers. Parents regularly request that their children be placed in the superstar's classroom.

A final, but critical, litmus test of superstars is that they are *respected* by all or almost all other faculty members. This is an important measure. It also implies that a superstar cannot be perceived as the "principal's pet." A superstar may in fact be the favorite teacher of the building administrator, but if other staff members perceive the relationship in that fashion, they may lose respect for, and even resent, the superstar. The superstar will sense this and then it is easy to foresee what will happen to this valuable faculty member's morale level.

A quick definition of superstars is that if they left your school, you probably would not be able to hire other teachers as good to replace them. It is also essential to realize that superstars want two things—autonomy and recognition. It's easy to see the challenge of finding a balance between the superstars' desire for autonomy and recognition and their need not to be perceived as receiving special attention from the leader. It is critical, though, to find this balance. Remember, the superstar can *be* the "pet" of the leader, but must not be *perceived* as such by the other staff members; that perception could potentially have a harmful effect on the superstar's morale. Regardless, it is still essential to make decisions based on your very best staff members. In a minute we will discuss why this is true, and Chapter 3 will provide some suggestions for how to accomplish this by using private versus public praising.

The second category of teachers is the **backbones**. Backbones are good, solid teachers, the heart of a faculty. They traditionally comprise 80 to 90 percent of your staff. They are good, stable, hardworking teachers. A quick determination of which teachers are backbones is that if two or three of your backbone teachers left the staff, you could probably do about as well in replacing them. You would consistently want to hire the rare superstar, but on a routine basis, when a backbone teacher left, you could hire someone who is about as effective. This is not an indictment of backbones; it is just a way to develop an understanding of their impact on the faculty dynamics.

To identify the third group, the **mediocres** (which may be too kind a word), ask yourself, "Which teachers, if they left the organization, could easily be replaced by a more effective teacher?" Our instinct when we think of increasing the morale of our school may be to focus on the most disgruntled faculty members, who may often be these mediocres; however, we must resist this temptation and choose a more productive approach.

Casey Stengel, the legendary baseball manager, used to describe leading a baseball team in this fashion. A manager has five players who love him, five players who hate him, and fifteen players sitting on the fence. The key to being a good manager is to keep the fifteen who are sitting on the fence from moving over to the side of the five who hate him.

Leading a school effectively may better be described as the process of getting the fifteen backbones onto the side with the superstars. Figuring out the most effective way to continue to enhance and develop the morale of the majority of your staff, the backbones and the mediocres, is an essential part of the role of an effective principal. The place to start, though, is with the superstar.

THE LEADERSHIP OF THE SUPERSTAR

The key for implementing change and growth in a building is to work with the superstar teachers in the school. If the superstars, the informal leaders, move forward, then the entire building has the opportunity to go with them. If they are not supportive of a change, then it is likely that the change will be minimally successful at best. This is also true of the morale of the school. I had a friend who would say about her family, "If Mama ain't happy, ain't nobody happy." The same can be said about the superstars of our organization and their influence on others; if the key informal leaders are unhappy, then everybody is unhappy.

When we think of our own organization, we can easily think of teachers who sort into each of the three groups: superstars, backbones, and mediocres. Though not all informal leaders come from the superstar category, it is a good place to start in determining the potential change agents in a school. And changing the morale of an organization is similar to implementing any type of change.

Let's look at an example. One of the schools where I was principal was a very old and unattractive building. Though this was not easy to alter, I felt that the classrooms could be much more attractive and inviting in appearance. I believe that every classroom should look like the best kindergarten classroom you have ever seen. In other words, it should look inviting, feel comfortable, and have student work displayed all over. Well, my school was quite the opposite and I wondered what to do. I was pretty sure that issuing a memo was not going to have any great effect, so I found a school, an older facility like mine, whose classrooms looked the way I wanted mine to look—alive, attractive, and very inviting.

I took three of my superstar teachers with me to a meeting at this school, and I parked at the far end of the building. The entire time we were at the meeting, the teachers kept asking me,

"Why are we here?" because the meeting did not have much to do with them. Finally, when the meeting ended, we walked out of the meeting room toward the car. I stopped at the first room we walked by and went in. I said excitedly, "Look at this room! This is great!" Well, the three superstars, "bored to the gourd" because of the meeting, grudgingly looked in the classroom and their eyes started to gleam. Then I went into the next room and said, "This one is even better!" My teachers began to have some spring in their step and soon started leading me around, and excitedly they went in every classroom in the school. On the way home, they could not stop talking about how attractive and inviting all of the classrooms were. Well, this happened on a Thursday. On Monday, what do you think the three superstars' classrooms looked like? Their classrooms did not just emulate the classrooms we had seen the previous week—they looked even better!

In my next weekly staff memo, the Friday Focus, I wrote, "Has anybody been in Mary's, Nancy's, or Jackie's rooms lately? Wow! No wonder the kids love their classes. When I went into their classrooms I wanted to bring a sleeping bag and stay all night!"

All of my teachers, cooks, custodians, bus drivers—the whole staff—received the Friday Focus. What do you think they did the day they read it? Every person in the school went by Mary's, Nancy's, and Jackie's rooms to see what they looked like. Even more important, other teachers started to change their classrooms' appearance to look like Mary's, Nancy's, and Jackie's.

Contrast this to what would have happened had I taken a couple of backbone teachers or even mediocre teachers with me to that other school. If they had looked at those classrooms on Thursday, what would theirs have looked like on Monday? Probably they would have looked the same. But even if one of them had changed their rooms, what effect would it have had on anyone else in the school? It is not very likely that it would have been as dramatic as the superstar teachers' impact.

Understanding the dynamics and relations in a school is one of the essential elements in successfully working to improve any aspect of the school—especially morale. Though the goal of this book is to enhance the morale of all staff, it is beneficial to keep in mind which of the three categories describes each of your staff members.

Another way to look at the importance of the informal leaders is to think of the influence they have on others. If an informal leader thinks that something is a bad idea, think of how many others this may impact. (And in the case of superstar teachers, if they think something is a bad idea, there is a good chance that it is.)

AUTONOMY OF THE SUPERSTAR—
AN IMPORTANT INGREDIENT OF SUCCESS

It is valuable to understand the application of autonomy to the superstars. To preserve this autonomy, we should avoid trying to control the behavior of less effective staff by implementing rules. The problem is that although the intent of the new rule is to alter the behavior of our more negative influences, the people most likely to follow it are the superstars. By following the rule, they will lose some autonomy. Therefore, we must look for other means of working with our mediocres and other difficult staff members.

When deciding whether to implement a new policy or "rule," give yourself a quick three-question quiz to determine whether this policy is likely to have a positive or a negative effect:

1. **What is my *true* purpose in implementing this rule or policy?**

2. **Will it actually accomplish this purpose?**

3. **How will my most positive and productive people feel about this policy?**

This sounds very basic, and it is; however, it can be not only a powerful measure of future policies, but also a help in determining the value of current procedures. Let us apply these questions to a scenario that is very common in many schools. Parents, guests, and others who come to the school encounter a sign in bold type:

ALL VISITORS MUST REPORT TO THE OFFICE!

This is a common front-door greeting. Using the three questions posed earlier, let's examine the impact of this expectation.

1. What is my *true* purpose in implementing this rule or policy?

Our instinctual reaction may be, "We want all visitors to go to the office and sign in, so that we can be aware of who is in the building." No doubt that this could be one reason. However, the underlying reason is to prevent someone from entering our school secretly and harming or abducting a student. This is a valiant aim, yet is this likely to be the result?

2. Will it actually accomplish this purpose?

The obvious answer to this question is "no." Someone attempting to do harm to a student or faculty member in the school is not going to be dissuaded by a sign on the front door. A person who brings a weapon into the school is not likely to "check the gun at the office," so to speak. In actuality, this sign is not likely to accomplish its intended positive purpose.

Even if the answer to question two is "yes" or even "maybe," this still does not mean that this new idea should be implemented. We need to weigh any potentially positive result on our difficult visitors (or staff members) against any harm that may result to our positive people. So this brings us to the third question:

3. How will my most positive and productive people feel about this policy?

A sign on the front door of a store says in bold print, "All Shoplifters Will Be Prosecuted!" Does this make you feel warm and welcome in the store? Do you think that this actually prevents someone who is planning on breaking the law from stealing in the store? Obviously not. Although the sign makes all the store's customers uncomfortable, the people who are its intended target will most likely ignore it or laugh at it.

This same effect is likely to occur in our schools. Ordering someone to do something is never a positive approach. Additionally, the sign described above is a reminder to the supportive parents who enter the school that something bad could happen to their children at school. We have chosen to place the feelings of our positive and supportive people below the hoped-for effect of a rule that will not work anyway.

As building leaders, we often state that we wish more parents and community members would become involved in the school. By our actions, we may be sending another more negative message. Realizing that this sign has no effect on intruders and has a negative effect on the vast majority of people who enter our school each day (including setting a negative smart-aleck tone for the students), we should reexamine what we do. We could accomplish the desired result to the same degree by keeping our positive supporters in mind:

**Welcome parents and visitors! We are glad you are here.
We do ask that all parents, visitors, and guests
sign in at the office.
Thank you for visiting Smith Middle School.**

The final support we need to offer is directions to the office. After all, if they are visitors, they probably do not know how to get there.

With this scenario in mind, we can apply these same three questions to the rules and procedures we attempt to implement in order to control our less reliable staff members. Are they likely to have an appropriate and positive effect on our school?

A couple of common scenarios that arise in schools are that teachers use the copier too much, or use supplies (folders, Post-It Notes, paper, and the like) at a frequency which will exceed the budget. Our instinct is to think that there are most likely a few people who are using things in an inappropriate manner or maybe even for personal use. As a result we are tempted to implement much stricter restrictions on using the copier or accessing supplies. We may require that all staff sign a piece of paper indicating how many copies they use. Or we might have all staff sign up on a list when they take any supplies. We may even issue a memo expecting staff to reduce their usage of copies or supplies. This is kind of a "guilty-until-proven-innocent" approach. We can apply our three rules and determine if this approach is appropriate.

1. What is my *true* purpose in implementing this rule or policy?

The purpose of putting forth this rule is to prevent those

people who are wastefully using the copier or taking too many supplies from continuing these practices.

2. Will it actually accomplish this purpose?

If people are doing something that is inappropriate, they most likely already know it is inappropriate and they just choose to do what they want. No one is under the assumption that it is *okay* to run copies of their Christmas card letter on the school copier. Some people, however, will do so at any opportunity. However, this is very few people. Is this likely to prevent the inappropriate usage of materials? Probably not. Even if the answer is maybe or yes, we still need to examine the potential result on our most important staff members—those who already follow these standards, even before a rule is implemented. Thus we will attempt to answer the third question, which is often the most important.

3. How will my most positive and productive people feel about this policy?

High achievers, which include your superstars and most effective teachers, are often very guilt-driven. They are likely to assume that any time a new rule or procedure is implemented, it could be because they have done something wrong. When you share with the staff that the copier is being used too much, the high achievers think to themselves about that time three years ago when they ran 25 copies for an activity and ended up needing only 22. They are the faculty members most likely to restrict their use of materials or supplies. Is this going to have a productive effect on the school? If you could give any one staff member an extra $250 for materials and supplies, which teacher would you be most confident would use this in a manner beneficial to students? The answer is the same superstars who are most likely to reduce their use of materials and supplies when a blanket "rule" is implemented.

Restricting the creativity of our most effective teachers will seldom have a positive effect. If you, as principal, wonder how your most effective faculty will receive a new expectation, the simplest method is to ask them before you implement the policy. Superstars generally will tell you the truth and not be a part of the rumor mill in a school. If they become involved in the spreading of gossip and rumors, they will lose respect and not remain superstars. Thus, asking them in advance how they would feel about a new procedure can help answer question three before it can negatively impact your most valuable staff members' morale.

Treating all teachers as if they want to do what is right can have positive effects on everyone, including our most challenging staff members. Let us examine another typical situation. In schools that have bells and passing times, principals often hope that teachers will supervise the hallways between classes. However, as people get busy, involved in other things, or maybe just unwilling, the people supervising the hallways may not be as great in numbers as the principal would like. A typical approach to getting more teachers to be in the hallway is to write a memo to all staff or make an announcement at the next faculty meeting. This approach often consists of language such as this: "A responsibility of every teacher in the school is to supervise the hallways between each class! It is important that everyone be in the hall during passing time. I know that some of you are not. It is in the teachers' handbook, so between every class you should be supervising." Just how effective is this approach?

1. Recall the three questions we described earlier:
2. What is my *true* purpose in implementing this rule or policy?
3. Will it actually accomplish this purpose?
4. How will my most positive and productive people feel about this policy?

Let us use these same three questions to analyze the effectiveness of our approach to enforcing a policy. What is the principal's true purpose? The true goal is to have more teachers supervise the hallways. Assume this issue is being addressed at a staff meeting; let us think through the effect of this approach.

If a staff consists of superstars, backbones, and mediocres, which of these groups is most likely to be supervising the hallways already? *The superstars.* Which of these three groups is least likely to be supervising the hallways already? *The mediocres.* One more review question: which of these groups is most important?

The superstars. With that in mind, let us proceed to the staff meeting. At table A is a group of mediocres. At table B is a group of superstars. The principal gives the following monologue to the entire staff.

"You teachers need to be in the hallways between classes! It is in the handbook and it is an expectation for everyone in this school. Two kids got in a fight today because no one was in the hallway. I expect each of you there every day!"

Now remember, the goal is to get teachers to be in the hallway more. After this lecture, how do the mediocres feel? They probably feel indifferent, or mad—or they were not even paying attention. Are they more likely to be in the hallway tomorrow? Probably not.

After this lecture, how do the superstars, who have been in the halls between classes, feel? They may wonder why you are talking to them, and they might feel frustrated and probably angry. Are they more likely to be in the hallway tomorrow? Probably not; and even if they are, they might be disgruntled about it.

Now we will rewind and start the faculty meeting over. At table A is a group of mediocres. At table B is a group of superstars. The principal addresses the entire staff in a sincere and yet gentle tone:

"I know how busy each of you is here at school. Everyone's plate is so full. But I want to take a minute out and thank those of you who take that extra effort to step out into and supervise the hallways between each class. I know your time is precious; however, it does make a big difference. Today I happened to be in a hallway in which two students were about to fight. One of them noticed a teacher nearby. I do not even think the teacher saw them. The student who saw the teacher pointed him out to his potential combatant. They then went their separate ways. I sincerely want to thank each of you who takes that extra effort to help make our school a safer place. It is much appreciated."

Now remember once again, the goal is to get teachers to be in the hallway more. After this lecture, how do the mediocres feel? Perhaps they feel guilty; they might be wishing they had received the attention; possibly they are indifferent. Often, many of them will feel pretty uncomfortable. The question is, are they more likely to be in the hallway tomorrow? Some are more likely to be in the hallway; for others, there may not be any difference. But remember, these are your least important people.

After this lecture how do the superstars who have been in the halls between classes feel? They are likely to feel proud, valued, and appreciated. Are they more likely to be in the hallway tomorrow? They are much more likely to help supervise the hallways. Keep in mind that as leaders, we strive to make decisions based on how our positive faculty will receive them.

Interestingly, a leader does not have to guess how superstars will react to an idea. If you ask them, they will tell you the truth. And, generally, superstars have the ability to tell you the truth in a way that you can accept, i.e., a way that is not offensive. This skill is one of the reasons that they are respected by their peers. And, if you have a question, the superstars generally have a good answer. They also have a vision that allows them to see things from a global perspective.

If leaders are not confident in their own skills or decision-making abilities, they do not want superstars in their organization. The reason is very simple. They are aware that the superstar knows whether they made a good decision or a poor one. If you do not have confidence in yourself, then this is the last person you want around.

However, if a leader can just have the confidence to tap into the superstars' resources of skills, they can be of great assistance. Remember, it's important to do this with enough subtlety that the superstar is not singled out. However, often the superstar is the first one to arrive at work, the last to leave, or both. So, there are probably many ways to use their services discreetly. No matter what approach a leader takes in getting assistance from the superstar, it is critical to understand the essential role that superstars play in affecting the morale of the entire school.

The focus of all educational leaders must first be on our most positive faculty members. Understanding and utilizing this dynamic is an essential step to developing positive morale for all staff.

3

RAISE THE PRAISE— MINIMIZE THE CRITICIZE

I truly believe that "Raise the Praise—Minimize the Criticize" should be not only the belief system for all educators at work, but also our guiding principle for life. It is critical that we operate from this perspective every day. Consistently taking a positive approach is a central element in establishing and enhancing the morale of those we work with. Looking for, acknowledging, and reinforcing the many positive things that occur in our organization may be the single most essential factor in cultivating positive morale. I want to share a story of how that became my approach as an educator.

LET'S GET THOSE KIDS LINED UP!

My first year as a teacher, I visited an elementary school during the spring of the year. I went to this K–6 school on a warm Friday afternoon in May—late May, to be exact. The school was an older building with a simple design. It had one hallway—kind of a shotgun-shaped school. Each grade level had two sections directly across the hall from each other. So, as you entered the long hallway, first there were two kindergarten classrooms, then two first grade, then two second grade, on down to the two sixth grade classes. And the teachers, all at the same time, were attempting to have their students line up in that hallway to go to an assembly the students were really excited about. Picture for a moment what those "lines" looked like on this warm Friday afternoon in May. You may be envisioning an amoeba, or a Slinky. As you can well imagine, getting those excited students to stand in an orderly fashion was quite a challenge.

Well, I walked into that school by the kindergarten classrooms and was heading toward the far end of the hall. As I walked into the building, I heard the teachers say loudly, "Jimmy, get your hands off Billy!"; threateningly, "Kevin, do you not want to go to the assembly?"; and exhaustedly, "I've told you at least a dozen times!"

You can imagine the lack of impact that this verbal lambasting had. And every teacher sounded the same, and every group of students looked more like a wet noodle than a line. But, out of the corner of my eye, at the far end of the hallway, I saw a sixth grade class that was lined up straight as an arrow. I remember thinking to myself, " I wonder what that teacher is *doing* to those kids?" How could she get them in such straight lines? I assumed she must have been a drill sergeant. She had to have been to get the kids lined up so straight. But when I got down to her class I heard something that I have never forgotten.

I heard that petite mild-mannered teacher say, "Susan, I really appreciate the way you are standing so straight and tall and leading our group. Johnny, you and Billy are directly behind one another—thank you. Jim, you are doing an outstanding job of staying in line." Those students could not wait to hear these words of praise from their teacher.

I thought at length about what I had witnessed that day, and then I realized how important it is to consistently emphasize the positive. It is **essential** that educational leaders constantly work to raise the praise and minimize the criticize, not just some of the time, but in everything we do. Now, you might be thinking that this positive stuff works for elementary children, but not for adults. Let's look at another example.

EVERYBODY'S BEEN ON A DIET

I'm quite sure that all of us have been on a diet a one time or another. (I now call them "alternative eating plans.") Sometimes we have had success and other times we have fallen short of our goals. Usually we start out with great enthusiasm, but often this momentum wanes, sooner rather than later. So, I want you to ask yourself a question. Which is more likely to keep you on a diet—someone saying, "Boy, you are really looking good!" or the comment, "It's about time . . ."?

We are never too old to hear praise. Maybe the form needs to be different; we may be conscious of what others think when we get recognized; but it still feels good. When was the last time someone told you, or gave you a note that said, how much you are appreciated? If you can remember, do you recall how good you felt? Now, did that make you work harder, or slack off? Of course, it gave you a real boost. Realizing this can help us to focus on raising the praise. After all, every one of us has been on a diet.

FIVE THINGS THAT HELP PRAISE WORK

One of the challenges that all educators face is learning how to praise. That may seem silly, but often teachers have spent their whole careers looking for what is wrong, pointing out errors, and focusing on mistakes. This is a part of being an educator. However, an educational *leader* looks for opportunities to find people doing things right. One of the difficulties for many educators is truly understanding praise and being able to apply it on a daily basis.

Ben Bissell (1992) has described five things that help praise work—elements that are important if attempts at praise are to have the most positive effect possible. These five characteristics of effective praise are that it is **authentic, specific, immediate, clean,** and **private.** Let us apply these general characteristics to the specifics of motivating and praising teachers.

Authentic means that we are praising people for something genuine, recognizing them for something that is true. This is an important facet because the recognition of something authentic can never grow weary. Sometimes people state that they do not praise more because they feel that it will lose its credibility or that it will become less believable if it happens too much. The way to prevent this is to make sure that it is always authentic. No one ever feels that they are praised too much for something genuine. Authentic does not mean that it is earth-shattering or that it is a magnificent accomplishment. Instead, the only requirement is that it be true. As educational leaders, we have many opportunities to catch people doing things right. Remembering them, writing them down, and then sharing them with the person you are praising is an important facet of praising.

Second, effective praise is **specific**. The behavior we acknowledge often becomes the behavior that will be continued. If we can recognize teachers' positive efforts with specific recognition, then we can help them see specific areas of value. For example, acknowledging that a teacher did an effective job of using questioning skills during a class period that you dropped in to informally observe can help reinforce this teaching style. Specific praise also allows you to reinforce someone in an authentic manner. If you use specific praise, you can recognize everyone in your organization. Even teachers that are struggling can still be praised. You do not have to be dishonest and say a person is an outstanding teacher, or that a particular lesson was excellent, if they were not. Instead, you can identify those areas that did have merit and acknowledge them through praise.

The third item is **immediate**. This means recognizing positive efforts and contributions in a timely manner. Providing authentic and specific feedback in close proximity to when it occurs is an important element in making reinforcement effective. One tactic that allowed me to give efficient feedback when doing informal "drop-in" supervision (Glatthorn 1984) to several classes in a row was to take a memo pad with me. If I visited eight classes for two to five minutes each, I would remain in the last class and write specific words of praise for each of the eight teachers, assuming that there was something I could authentically reinforce. When I returned to the office, I would ask the secretary to put them in the teachers' mailboxes. Other principals carry Post-It Notes with them and put them on the door when they leave each individual class. For even more immediate feedback, they could also place them on the teacher's desk, grade book, or lesson plan book. I would work very hard to find something positive in teachers' classrooms, as often as possible. It could be related to the topic, what students were saying or doing, the physical environment, or even a new tie a teacher was wearing. Positive reinforcement is a valuable tool for change.

The fourth guideline for praise is that it be **clean**. This is often a very challenging expectation, especially for educators. Clean means a couple of different things.

First, praise is not clean if you are issuing it in order to get the teacher to do something in the future. In other words, it is important to compliment someone because it is authentic, not just because you are hoping that they will do something different—and unrelated—tomorrow. Take care to remind yourself of this quite regularly; otherwise, you will be tempted to discontinue praising because you feel it "did not work." For example, during the morning you might praise a less positive staff member for the "wait time" they were using in class; later in the day, that teacher might be less than friendly to you. Do not feel that these two events are linked. Oftentimes we take the unprofessional manner of less positive people very personally. Though our goal is to get them to be more positive, we need to be aware that often their mood has much more to do with them and the way they feel about themselves than it does with you and how they are regarding you.

The second aspect of clean praise is a very challenging one for educators. If praise and reinforcement is to be clean, it cannot include the word "but." If we are trying to compliment someone and we say, "I appreciated the tone of voice you were using with Steven today, but I also noticed you haven't changed your bulletin boards lately," the individual we hoped to praise will very likely remember only the part after the "but"—which was a criticism. If we are really intending to praise someone, then it is important that we separate these two comments. The statement "I appreciated the tone of voice you were using with Steven today" could have been an authentic, specific, immediate, positive, and reinforcing event for this teacher. Such a statement helps to clarify and reinforce your expectations about how students in the school are to be treated. It also makes it much more likely that the teacher will consciously seek to address students in this manner in the future.

The other part of the comment, "you haven't changed your bulletin boards lately," should be given at another time and in another way. Tying the two together reduces or even eliminates the value of the praise. Building the morale of others requires a consistent focus on looking for positive things. Any time the opportunity presents itself, acknowledging the good appropriately can continue to cultivate a positive mindset among others.

The fifth descriptor of praise is **private**. Dr. Bissell believes that the vast majority of the time, praise needs to be given in private. I agree with this and would also say that if in doubt, you are always safe to praise someone in private.

One reason is to protect the feelings of our productive backbones and superstars. As we mentioned in Chapter 2, it is a delicate balance to make sure that the most productive staff members are not resented by others. Also, because of the concept of the Comparison Other, praising less productive staff members publicly can be a demotivator for positive staff. If I see a person whom I view as less hardworking get public recognition, I may lower my effort level to regain the balance between my efforts and my rewards. However, there are still times when it is beneficial to use public praise to influence others and build morale. Let's examine some situations.

PUBLIC VERSUS PRIVATE PRAISING

Understanding the difference in impact between recognizing someone's efforts publicly and acknowledging them privately is very important. In the previous chapter we discussed the delicate balance between giving superstars recognition and building up resentment toward them by other faculty members. To be effective, a leader must know when to praise publicly and when to praise privately.

If we never recognize accomplishments publicly, however, we may lose many teachable moments. Think back to my example of taking three superstars to a meeting at a school whose classrooms presented a positive appearance. The superstars were inspired to "upgrade" their own classrooms over the next weekend, which of course was a benefit to our school and particularly to those three classes. Of course, as mentioned earlier, those three superstars' classrooms probably needed the least improvement of any in the school. But when I gave those teachers *public* recognition in the Friday Focus, other teachers became involved as well; eventually, these changes positively influenced even some of my mediocre teachers. Without this avenue of public praise, the impact would have been much more limited.

Keep in mind, too, that superstars thrive on autonomy and recognition, although this recognition does not necessarily mean only public acknowledgments. When considering the public praising of staff members, however, remember that one of the most important facets of being a superstar is being respected by others, including peers. So be aware of the amount of public recognition you give your superstars, especially if positive reinforcement is somewhat new to your school climate and culture. If the other staff members become resentful, superstars are no longer superstars, and this is a dramatic limitation on their future ability to be a positive influence for the school.

An easy test of whether it is okay to praise in public is whether the praised behavior is something anyone *could* have done. Publicly recognizing a teacher who chooses to write a grant that will benefit the school is an example. Any staff member could have chosen to pursue a grant and thus could have received this recognition. As others choose to write grants, the leader has many other chances to recognize staff members— many other appropriate opportunities for positive reinforcement in an authentic, specific, immediate, clean, and public manner.

This same concept of public versus private praising is applicable to students. Recognizing students publicly when they achieve a 3.5 grade point average may seem reinforcing, but many of these students would rather receive private recognition; it may not be "cool" to have high grades. Realistically, we often have many students in our schools who could not have achieved this lofty GPA. Having a private ceremony for these "honor roll" students, or sending their parents a letter, would probably accomplish the same thing without potentially building resentment among their peers.

Another way to get the benefit of public praise without building animosity is by anonymously acknowledging a contribution using generalized public praise. This can allow for reinforcement and provide the desired "teachable moment" without as much potential for resentment. The example in Chapter 2 regarding hallway duty applies here. Publicly thanking "those of you who take that extra effort to step out into and supervise the hallways between classes" is a way to help people who have done this feel appreciated. At the same time, this can help establish an expectation for everyone to behave in this manner. You could also individually thank people you have seen in the hallway, or write notes acknowledging these efforts. However, this private acknowledgement alone will not likely get others to join them in this supervisory task.

A similar situation involves getting teachers to turn in their grades, supply orders, or any paperwork on time. Traditionally, we may issue reminders which can go from friendly encouragement to heavy-handed directives. However, using generalized public praise can allow us to reinforce the behavior of those who have met or exceeded the standard, while at the same time reminding others to "get with the program." Instead of saying for the fifth time in a memo, "the deadline for turning in grade sheets is today," an approach which would be just as effective and yet more reinforcing could be, "I appreciate those of you who have already turned in your grade sheets to the office. Turning them in before today's deadline helps our busy staff tremendously. Thanks for your efforts." This serves as a reminder to everyone and as a "thank you" to a few. Using the generalized public praise approach can also protect anyone who was a "rate buster" on the grade-sheet deadline.

Though the balance between publicly recognizing people for their efforts and potentially alienating them from their peers may be delicate, there are still many occasions when making praise public is important. Being aware of when it is best to praise publicly and when situations call for private acknowledgement is a valuable part of positively influencing morale. Developing tools like the Friday Focus (discussed at length in a later chapter) gives you the opportunity to choose which type of praising is most appropriate in a particular circumstance. However you elect to reinforce the efforts of others, it is essential that you "Raise the Praise!" on a regular basis.

PRACTICING THE PRAISE

Praise is valuable in that it can assist others. However, it is also a powerful tool that can be good for the praiser. When I was an assistant principal, I realized that it was up to me whether I was going to enjoy my job or not. If I just waited around for things to happen, they surely would. Unfortunately, most of the things that come the way of an assistant principal, the person responsible for discipline of 750 eighth graders, tend to be negative. I realized that I was going to deal with students when they were in trouble, teachers when they had a problem, and parents when they were upset. I then determined that it is *my* responsibility to meld my job so that it would be enjoyable to come to work each day. In order to try to maintain a little balance in my job, I started a **positive referral** program.

Most schools have discipline referrals; teachers "write up" kids for misbehavior and then send them to the office with the referral form. Assistant principals often deal with the majority of these situations. However, I felt that it was important to have a positive referral program. We created a form that was similar in format, only on bright red paper. Teachers would "write up" students for doing positive things. It could be that Tim got a B+ on a math quiz, that Juan helped a student who was on crutches move around the school for a week, or that her homeroom teacher enjoyed seeing Megan's smiling face every morning. As long as it was something authentic, it was appropriate to write up a positive referral and put it in my mailbox.

When I pulled the positive referral out of my mailbox, I would send for the student. Initially, students were nervous, frightened, or defensive when they were summoned to the office. Often students would walk in and immediately tell the secretary, "It wasn't me!" When I called the student into my office, I would first offer congratulations and say how proud I was. I would share which teacher made the referral, and why. I would thank the student for helping to make our school a better place.

This, in and of itself, may have been enough. However, I took it one step further. I would pick up the phone and call the child's parent. If there were two parents, I would call the one who worked outside the home. And if they both did, I would call the one who worked in the busiest office or on the most crowded factory assembly line. Let's think for a moment what those phone calls were like. Suppose I'm calling Kenny Johnson's mother at work about a positive referral.

"Hi, Mrs. Johnson, this is Bill Smith, assistant principal at Meadow Grove Middle School."

As you can imagine, this conversation was usually interrupted at this point by the parent with a loud moan, "Oh, no!"

I would then continue the conversation. "Mrs. Johnson, I hate to bother you at work, but I just thought you might want to know that Kenny's teacher, Mrs. Smith, is running around up here at school, bragging on your son. She sent me a positive referral saying that Kenny did an excellent job working with his group leading a science experiment yesterday. I called Kenny down to the office to congratulate him and I wanted to call and share the good news with you."

The conversation then typically would continue in a very positive manner. I would let the parent know that the student was in the office with me—"Would you like to talk with Kenny?"

A lot of principals have positive referrals and other programs in their schools. This is wonderful. However, the added twist of calling the parents at work led to several significant and positive contributions for me.

Interestingly, the most frequent comment I received from parents was, "A school has never called with anything good before." I called hundreds and hundreds of parents, and this was consistently the theme. It did not matter if I was contacting the parent of a student who was frequently in trouble or the future valedictorian. Parents had never had unsolicited, positive contact from anyone at school.

Though I thought this was very sad, it did help me realize a couple of things. First, I finally understood why people believe the criticism of schools and teachers they read in the newspapers, and why people buy into the nonsense that they hear on radio call-in shows criticizing educators and schools in America. It is because if they do not hear good news from us, the public may never hear *good* news about schools and teachers. Thus, it is critically important that we consistently initiate positive contact with parents.

At this point you may be asking yourself a couple of things. "Why did you call parents specifically at work?" and "This is all fine and dandy, but what does this have to do with building staff morale?" Well, let me take a stab at answering both those questions.

I called the parents at work for a very selfish reason. It relates to the publicity issue. When I called Mrs. Johnson and her initial reaction was a loud, "Oh, no!"—do you have any guess about the first thing she did in that crowded office when she hung up the phone? She told everybody in the office! And I don't know about you, but I do not mind people saying good things about me, my teachers, and my school in public. I also know there was an office full of other parents who were thinking to themselves that their child's school never has called with good news. Anything that builds the reputation of you, your faculty, or your school does nothing but help the morale of the staff.

Just imagine the impact on the relationship between the student and the teacher who wrote the referral. So many times, the student would go into the classroom the next day and thank the teacher, reporting excitedly something like "Mom was so happy, she took me out for pizza!" What a positive impact this had on teacher-student relations. As you can well imagine, the relationship between the teacher and the parents was also greatly enhanced.

Additionally, this whole process yielded a couple of selfish benefits for me. One of them arose if I had to call a parent at some future point with less than good news. If I had previously initiated positive contact, it is amazing how that impacted future calls. Suppose, several weeks after the first conversation, I have to call Mrs. Johnson about a discipline matter.

"Hi, Mrs. Johnson, this is Bill Smith, assistant principal at Meadow Grove Middle School."

And Mrs. Johnson would reply, "Hi. How are you today?"

At first, I was so shocked by Mrs. Johnson's friendly response that I would assume she had not understood me! But eventually I would continue:

"Mrs. Johnson, I hate to bother you at work, but today Kenny was involved in an incident where he was...(fighting, sent to the office, etc.) and as a result he will be receiving...(detention, suspension, etc.)."

Then, Mrs. Johnson would respond by using the "F" word on me. She would say, "That's okay. I know you're Fair. You call me with good news and you call me with bad news. You can call me anytime you want."

What I quickly learned was that making positive referrals

may have seemed like additional work, but it really made my job easier. I had built relationships with parents that had significant positive impacts down the line. My job just became more tolerable. However, the real benefit from making positive phone calls was even more selfish. Let's examine the most powerful result of these positive phone calls.

MY UNCLE LARRY

Who is it that determines how much we praise? Obviously, it is ourselves. We decide each day how much, if at all, we are going to use praise. I am glad that it is our own responsibility. Because if my Uncle Larry decided how much we praise, we never would. His theory is, "I don't want you going around smiling, ruining my bad day!" Do you know any folks like that? Not too pleasant, are they? Have you ever worked with anyone like that? Not much of a treat, is it? However, those folks do not praise anyone because they are so down on themselves and life that they do not want anyone else to be in a good mood. As a matter of fact, according to Ben Bissell (1992), the single biggest determinant of how much we praise is *how we feel about ourselves*. That is why we devote a later chapter of this book to the importance of taking care of yourself; if we do not take care of ourselves, there is not much chance we can take care of anyone else either.

So, what is my second selfish interest in making positive referral phone calls or utilizing any type of praise? Well, we determine how much we praise. And now, ask yourself a question. Any time you praise, at least how many people feel better? The answer, of course, is two. And one of those two people is always yourself. In other words, anytime *we* praise, *we* feel better!

That is why this is in the staff morale book. One of the best ways to build morale is to praise others. This is also one of the best ways to build your own morale! Now, how can you spread this school-wide?

Well, we had such a positive response from students, parents, and the community (even the newspaper wrote about it!) that the teachers decided to get personally involved. The teaching staff, when I became principal, decided that each teacher would make one positive phone call per week.

We realized that we also needed to dedicate a day to this. As all of us know, if we do not choose a particular day and write it down in our calendars and/or lesson plan books, we will most likely forget. So we chose Tuesday, and we called it "Terrific Tuesday."

Now, any cynics who are reading this book might be thinking, "What about those people who didn't call? Did anything happen to them?" My response is that I would not give them the power to ruin a great idea. My goal in a school is not perfection—it is improvement. If you have 30 teachers in your school and 20 of them start to make positive phone calls, is your school better off or worse off? Obviously, it is better off. And you cannot get everyone involved until you get someone involved. Additionally, this program is self-reinforcing. Once the teachers begin making positive calls, they feel better about themselves. Since they now feel better about themselves, they are even more likely to make calls in the future. And, if they make more calls, they feel even better. And since they feel even better…well, you get the picture. This is a very self-fulfilling prophecy once it gets started.

EVERY DAY IN EVERY WAY

We went into depth regarding the positive referral program and phone calls to help develop an understanding regarding the relationship between praise and morale. However, there are many ways to help boost the morale in your school. I mentioned making a round of informal drop-in visits, pausing in the last classroom to write positive notes to the teachers you observed. If you can do this on a daily basis, you have a quick and regular method of giving others a boost.

Maybe instead of phone calls, or in addition, each staff member can have a supply of postcards. The postcards can be bright and cheery. Around the outside they can say, "Great Job, Way to Go, Terrific, Outstanding, Excellent . . . ." The teachers can jot a little note about a student, and then the school can mail the postcard to the student's home.

Every school has numerous ways for praising others. The key to building morale in a school is for the leader consistently to recognize the efforts of everyone in the school and then model the praising for all to see. This approach is contagious in any organization. So, take care of yourself, and have fun!

4

ONE FOR ALL AND ALL FOR ONE—BUILDING A SHARED VISION

VISION—A GUIDE TO SUCCESS

Directions . . . everyone needs them. Accomplishing a task is much harder if there is no path to follow. Guiding someone to your house, baking a cake, assembling the new barbecue grill would all be difficult endeavors if directions weren't supplied. But sometimes directions aren't supplied, and the achievement of a goal becomes more difficult. These are the times when the collective efforts of many can lead to great success.

I recall back in my Scouting days when our troop participated in a competition during a camping retreat. We were competing against other troops to see who could perform basic camping chores the most efficiently. My task (along with two friends of mine) was to build a fire. I don't exactly remember how we got started, but eventually each one of us was supplying a necessary element to make the fire start. One friend was supplying and stacking wood, the other was providing the lighted match, and I had the illustrious job of blowing beneath the wood to help the match ignite our fire. Well, for those of you outdoor folks, you know that this process can take quite a while and at one point our "sort of fire" would produce only smoke, smoke that, of course, blew right at me. But I kept on huffing and puffing while the smoke caused tears to stream down my face, because I wanted to win . . . I wanted to accomplish a goal. The next thing I knew my leader was lifting me up and screaming that we won. My tears were now tears of joy. I found my campfire partners and we screamed and hugged as only 10-year-old Girl Scouts can do. We accomplished our goal collectively. We found that each of us could contribute and that contributing was fulfilling.

Principals must keep this in mind when deciding upon the vision, mission, or goals of the building. Everyone has a part to play, everyone can make their personal contribution, and everyone must *feel* that their contribution is important.

VISION—THE PERSONAL SIDE

Before we begin the daunting task of creating a shared vision within our organization, we must first look within ourselves. Leaders must have their belief systems well grounded and internalized before they can help a group move toward a shared vision. What do you, as an educational leader, believe about schooling? As we search within for the answer to this question, we realize that what emerges is very personal. When I delve into my thoughts and memories, isolated stories and incidents begin to surface:

- ◆ The time my mean fourth grade teacher cried as she read the final pages of *Old Yeller.*

- ◆ The time I stood in the corner in first grade for crossing my arms and huffing because I couldn't sit by my best friend.

- ◆ The time the teacher asked Dan E. to take a paper towel and wipe his teeth. (He never brushed them.)

- ◆ The time the sixth-grade bully cornered me in the bathroom and I escaped within an inch of my life.

- ◆ The time I wore my beautiful purple dress to school in hopes that Donny B. would fall in love with me. (He did not.)

- The time I cut my hair so short in eighth grade I wore a cap to school all day.
- The first time I had to shower in P. E.
- The time that someone dared to pick on my little sister on the bus. (He lived to regret it.)
- The first time I sang a solo on stage. It was "You Make Me Feel Brand New" and my parents still have the twenty-year-old cassette.
- The time my sophomore English teacher read the poetry of James Whitcomb Riley aloud to us. I asked for a collection of his poems for Christmas.

This list could go on and on. These experiences as a student unknowingly began to create my vision of school. I became a teacher, and experiences again continued to shape my beliefs. I recall:

- The time I took my fifth graders out to the flagpole and sang "America the Beautiful."
- The many times I read *The Chronicles of Narnia* to my students.
- Attempting in vain to teach possessives to my third graders with the textbook. We finally wrote a jingle that helped us remember what to do with that *dreaded* apostrophe.
- The principal's face the time I brought two vigilantes to the office for praise and not punishment.
- The moment in time when Deanna P. learned what italics were.
- The parent/teacher conference when I shared with Andrew K.'s parents (through a mist of tears) that he *was* a learner.
- The joy of reading and using the mighty works of Chris Van Allsburg.
- The last day of school with the very first class I ever taught. Enough said.

I became a principal. Fond memories make me smile....

- ◆ The mornings of greeting our smiling students at the front door.
- ◆ The tireless and positive staff that surrounded me each and every day.
- ◆ The day we learned we won the National Blue Ribbon Award.
- ◆ The time Bobby S. shared with me that his momma was gonna come and tear the school down brick by brick and bury me alive with them.
- ◆ The tears I shed after viewing the rat-infested trailer park where Bobby S. lived.

These many experiences have molded how I see school and what I want the business of school to be about. Keep in mind that I now work at an institution of higher learning and my vision continues to grow and take on a different structure because of my experiences. I am a parent of three children. School through the lens of a parent adds an additional complex dimension to what I believe schools should look and act like. Throughout my personal and professional life I have had many encounters with the world of education. These encounters have shaped my passion for this, the most noble profession of all.

Leaders must have their own well-grounded beliefs about how learning is best facilitated. This does not imply that the leader must inflict that vision on the school, but that the leader's belief system must be in place so that the school and its leader can find mutual ground on which to build. This is the only way that progress and success can occur. As a leader, ask yourself what your vision is. What is it that matters most to you? Can you articulate this? It is essential that we develop, refine, and when appropriate, be able to communicate our educational vision.

VISION—A MUST FOR EACH TEACHER

Teachers must be encouraged to create a personal vision for themselves. We talk often about the vision of the school and its leader, but we oftentimes don't give enough attention to the vision of each staff member. How can we encourage and help each teacher find their own personal place in the world of education? We tell them that their job is to meet the individual needs of every child in their classroom. It is in this same fashion that we, as leaders, must strive to look at each teacher as an individual. It is our obligation to celebrate what they can bring to our school and cultivate their strengths.

The simplest way to make teachers feel that they contribute is to make pointed contact with them each and every day. This means being in their classrooms and truly noticing what is taking place. Have specific conversations about what you saw. Note innovative strategies they are using and tell them you noticed. This could be accomplished face to face, in a written note, or via e-mail. These strategies will be expanded upon in Chapter 7.

Teachers must have the opportunity to articulate their personal beliefs and where they want this belief system to lead them. Many principals are wonderful about providing staff members an individual meeting with them when they first become the new leader of the school. These meetings are just to talk and share thoughts about past years and hopes for coming years. Perhaps an individual meeting with each teacher at the beginning of the year should be an annual occurrence. This is not a meeting with a lot of structure, just a meeting to talk and make sure that the teacher knows you are listening. Help them begin to articulate what they hope to accomplish this year on a professional level. Ask them how the school and you can help them achieve these goals. Whether you are a principal, department chair, superintendent, or grade-level leader, regular conversations with everyone you lead can have a significant, positive impact on your organization.

VISION—LET'S GROW ONE

Each faculty member has their belief system and vision in place. It is at this point that the vision of the school can begin to evolve and unfold. Pulling together into one vision becomes easier when all stakeholders feel confident in their contribution. There are many different routes to a vision. Developing a vision is a complicated process that cannot be achieved in a two- or three-hour faculty meeting. Roland Barth (1993) states that "a vision is a kind of moral imagination which gives school people, individually and collectively, the ability to see their school not only as it is, but as they would like it to become" (p. 10). Many schools can articulate what they do, but forget to add the integral part about what they want to become. Barth then shares that "the most hopeful and ambitious means by which a school comes to have a vision is to grow one" (p. 10).

This vision growth involves members of the school community as they design a process for examining their school. They look at "what it is and isn't doing for the little people and the big people" (p. 10). With this information, they begin to create a vision that provides a sense of purpose for the organization and also for the individual members within it. This vision will reflect what is currently productive and successful in the school, but also included will be the promising ideas for the future. A next step, but an important one, involves the fertilization of the school soil so that the vision can grow and flourish. Once the vision is determined, the school leader must locate the necessary nutrients to enrich the sod in which the vision was so carefully created and planted. This growth and building process is not the easiest route to a vision, but the most successful for long-term growth and internalization of what is best for the school.

Usually the gathering together of stakeholders, brainstorming what we do well and what we want to in the future, and articulating a written vision from this is a relatively painless process. It takes time, planning, and energy, but is a very doable task. The part that is often neglected is the follow-up to the vision. Educational leaders must regularly reflect upon the vision and ask themselves if they are doing everything in their power to make this vision a reality for the members of the learning community. Are they nourishing the vision properly and continuously now that it is planted?

THE PRINCIPAL—THE VISION ROLE MODEL

One aspect of perpetuating the vision now that it is in place must emanate from the principal. The leader must never forget that it is imperative to model this vision visibly in words and actions. These actions must constantly reflect the belief system of the school. If your school believes that respect for self, others, and the environment is a part of your vision, then you must live by this as you have cafeteria duty with one hundred first and second graders. You must live by this when a ninth grader tells you to f— off. You must live by this when the custodian doesn't have the gym ready for the 2:00 assembly. You must live by this when one of your teachers disagrees with your schedule changes. Living the vision can be difficult. It sometimes requires patience and professionalism of superhuman lengths, but this is your job. You set the standard of excellence in the school, and everyone is watching how you handle these tedious situations.

The following are some quotations from principals who were asked how they model the school's vision and beliefs on a daily basis:

- "If you can't be on time, be early."
- "Look for improvement, not perfection, in students and staff."
- "Never ask teachers to do anything I'm unwilling to do."
- "Help chip ice off the front steps on snowy days."
- "Take classes and share the information you learn."
- "Dress professionally *every* day."
- "Try to always have a 'ready smile'."
- "Always treat teachers as I would expect them to treat children."
- "Don't ever gossip with the staff."
- "Admit mistakes."
- "Don't talk during staff meetings."
- "Greet individuals with a smile and call them by name."
- "Pick up the stray paper in the hallways and throw it away."
- "Don't be afraid to laugh."
- "WALK THE TALK."

Your modeling can provide the greatest inspiration and teaching to your students, staff, and parents. It also keeps the focus and meaning of the vision front and center for everyone. Modeling the vision is the most important thing you do each day. At the end of the day when you haven't returned a single phone call and the paperwork is still stacked a mile high in front of you, ask yourself what you did accomplish. If you can say that you were a positive role model for all you encountered...you did your job completely.

I close this section with some quotes from *Improving School from Within*, by Roland Barth. Some of his thoughts on school vision:

- Vision unlocked is energy unlocked (p.151).
- To become a good school requires a change of vision from within (p.151).
- A school without vision is a vacuum inviting intrusion (p.152).
- In schools treading water is no longer an option. School people must either propel themselves in some direction, be towed, or sink (p. 152).
- The Old Testament tells us "a people without a vision shall perish." The same can be said about schools and school people without visions. It might also be said that schools full of vision will flourish (p. 160).

Creating and perpetuating a shared vision is the beginning of a noble and realistic journey for a school. The role of the school leader is to foster the creation of the vision, plant it carefully in rich soil, nourish the soil continuously, and watch the vision prosper and thrive.

PARTICIPATIVE MANAGEMENT—
GETTING EVERYONE INVOLVED

As the professionalism of educators increases and the expectations placed on school leaders continue to compound, principals have looked to involve more people in the decision-making process of a school. The influx of site-based management schools has also added to the need for a higher level of participation by the teaching staff. This is commonly referred to as participative management.

The Duluth Public Schools implemented a participative management process on a district and school level. Moeser and Golen (1987) defined participative management as "an attitude and a management process that involves employees in decisions that affect the delivery of services" (p. 3). Moeser and Galen felt participative management allowed the district the advantage of better meeting the mission of the district.

Participative management had been operative in Duluth on an informal basis for years in the form of staff input in the budgeting process, individual school senates, staff input in determining building-level objectives, and various advisory committees. In an effort to have more uniform usage of participative management, the policy of the district changed to encourage "employee involvement and participation in problem-solving and decision-making" (p. 6).

For the Duluth School District, excellence in management required management that (1) encourages participation and creativity among staff, (2) builds commitment to shared goals, (3) structures employee involvement so employees are routinely involved in decisions that affect them, (4) sets a high priority on advocating for ideas generated by subordinates, and (5) develops a strong sense of trust and collegiality among all staff members in the pursuit of the goal of excellence (p. 6).

Garten and Valentine (1989) stated that "effective instructional leadership depends on the principal's success in involving the faculty members in developing a shared vision of where the school should head and agreement on the procedures to move toward those goals" (p. 1).

Garten and Valentine described three strategies designed to involve faculty in effective schooling:

1. Use current and upcoming opportunities regularly and fully. This strategy involved using the regular post-observation conferences with teachers as a way to increase teacher involvement with the instructional concerns of the school.

2. Build your faculty members' knowledge of effective schools/teaching research and their skill in better identifying it in their teaching. This strategy involved the distribution of a summary of effective schools and effective teaching research.

3. Apply practical ideas on staff development/inservice. This strategy involved an attitude of development of professionalism among the teaching staff followed by needs assessment. Then faculty members should be involved in the prioritizing of the needs and the staff development process (pp. 1–3).

Lagana (1989) examined the management of change and school improvement as his basis for advocating employee participation. The author defined empowerment as "the process of providing people with the opportunity and necessary resources to enable them to believe and feel that they understand their world and have the power to change it; for example, greater autonomy and independence in decision making" (p. 52).

Lagana felt that educators must be trained to take risks. He stated that teachers might not be comfortable with empowerment. Lagana provided a list of conditions that promote change and school improvement:

1. Administrators must believe that teachers can identify and define their own professional development needs; and teachers have the potential to grow into expanded roles as more inquiring and contributing professionals.

2. Teachers must have appropriate time, occasions, and space for professional work and reflection.

3. Teachers must have training, follow-up, and technical assistance provided by respected persons. They also need ongoing coaching and feedback by credible persons.

4. Access to resources is important, as is sufficient money for the hiring of substitutes or paraprofessionals to cover non-teaching duties so that teachers can

spend more time in planning, reflection, and development.

5. Attention to teacher salaries for a longer school year is needed, as well as consultants and evaluators and a budget for curriculum projects and unexpected expenditures.

6. Teachers and the teachers' union must be committed to empowerment and the acceptance of greater accountability for school improvement efforts (pp. 53–54).

A commitment by the principal to use participative management is essential in order for staff input and participation to be effective. Martin and McGee (1990) discussed administrative support as an essential element in promoting and developing participatory management. They stated that the support needed to be evidenced by (1) a belief in participatory management and in people, (2) an attitude that would lend itself to a willingness to be open to suggestions and to listen, (3) recognition of a need for improvement in the decision-making process, and (4) a willingness to give time and attention to the program (p. 10).

Participatory management varies greatly from school to school. The leadership style of the principal is a key element in the effectiveness and degree of teacher participation. Some schools have very structured models for staff input, and others rely on informal communications for all idea sharing.

GUIDED GOAL SETTING FOR GROUPS

Leaders continually share that they want the input of others in decision making. In addition, people indicate that they want to be involved in the decision-making process of their organizations. How this can best be accomplished is a challenge that all educational leaders face. Developing a model for setting goals is an important component of developing this type of organization-wide buy-in. There are many approaches that allow a leader to accomplish this. We want to share one concept that you can utilize or alter to fit the needs of your group. This method is effective and efficient, both of which are important guides for deciding how to involve the group in goal-setting. We will provide a step-by-step approach. The entire process, from start to finish, can be completed in approximately two hours.

1. Get all members of your organization together and divide them randomly into groups of four to six members.

2. Have flip charts or large sheets of paper for each group and provide them with markers. Also, have pads of Post-It Notes available for each participant. In other words, if you have five groups of six members each, you should have five flip charts/markers and 30 pads of Post-Its.

3. After dividing your organization into the small groups, ask each person to brainstorm *individually* and without discussion what they feel the goals of the organization should be. Each goal that they think of should be written on a separate Post-It Note. Do not worry at this point about long-term or short-term goals; that can come later. Give the people ten to twenty minutes to record each of their goals on an individual Post-It.

4. The members of each group should put their individual Post-Its up on the wall in a cluster. They do not need to worry about repetition or sorting the goals in any way at this point. Each member should read the notes from their own small groups.

5. Then do a carousel walk. This is an activity where everyone in the room rotates and reads all of the Post-Its from each of the other groups. It is called a carousel walk because the groups should all rotate in the same direction like a carousel (for example, the groups should all move clockwise). Each person should take a pen and pad of Post-Its along as the group rotates. Those who see any goals that they did not think of originally and that they would like to add to their group should write each additional goal on a separate Post-It.

6. When the members get back to their original start-ing point, they should put any new Post-It ideas they wrote while walking around up on the wall with their cluster. In addition, if they thought of any new ideas, these can be added also.

7. The groups will probably have quite a large number of ideas on the notes in their clusters. Now ask the groups to sort their Post-Its into common themes. Some groups will be able to put everything into three or four groupings; others will still have eight or ten. Any number is okay at this point. Some of the Post-It ideas will continue to stand alone. This is completely fine.

8. Now ask each group member to take three new Post-It Notes and make a star on them. These are their three votes. They are then to place their three star votes on the themes their groups have developed. They should use these stars to vote for the ones they feel are most important. They can put all three on one if they feel it is the overwhelming important idea, two on one and one on another, or each on a differ-ent theme. The purpose of this step is to reduce the number of themes each group has. Then, depending on the size of the small groups, the people should eliminate any themes that did not receive at least one star vote (two star votes if the groups are large).

9. Then ask each of the groups to write up the themes that got at least one vote (or two if that was your standard) into goal statements on a large flip chart or piece of paper. In other words, if their theme was around student climate and safety issues, have them write it in a sentence or so in a goal format. An ex-ample might be "To increase the student climate and safety in our building."

10. Then tape the large papers with the small-group goals on the wall next to each other. Ask each of the groups to share the goal statements that they have on the papers on the wall. After they are done sharing, ask

the entire group if they notice any common goals among the groups. The answer is always yes. Often, the goals of the groups are almost identical.

11. Then, either working together as a group or having representatives of each group do so at another time, have the goals compiled into one list. If every group had something related to student climate and safety, it should only be listed once on this overall compilation.

12. You may be done at this point, depending on how many goals you have. If you have three to five, you might want to stop. However, if you have more than that, you can do step 8 again by making stars and voting for the top three choices. Then you can drop the goals with the fewest votes. This step could also be done outside of a whole group meeting. You could develop a ballot where people vote for three goals in the same fashion or have people rank every goal.

13. After the final list of goals is developed, you can then sort them into short-term, longer-term, and so on and develop a specific action plan for each.

This is a relatively quick and painless way to involve everyone in the goal-setting process of your group or organization!

SHARE YOUR SUCCESSES!

One of the things an educational leader can do that will immediately set a positive tone to a meeting is to have people share their successes. A formal way to do this is to divide the group up randomly into small groups of four to seven people. Then ask people to brainstorm as a group and tell about any successes that they or anyone in the group has had as a school, individually, or within their department, team or grade level. Set some type of a time guideline—in other words, successes over the last year or two years. Record every idea on large chart paper. Believe me, most groups will need several sheets. Allow the groups 15 to 45 minutes to complete this activity, depending on the size of your groups.

Before you do any type of brainstorming activity I would encourage you to share the "rules of brainstorming" with the group. These rules are

1. **List every idea.**
2. **Don't discuss.**
3. **Don't judge.**
4. **Repetition is okay.**

This may seem basic, but if we do not establish these guidelines in advance, we will find that groups tend to bog down and brainstorming is hindered. Focus on quantity, not quality at this point. I always put up an overhead with these rules, remind the group of the rules, and then leave it up during the entire process.

After each group is done compiling, tape up all of the lists on the walls around the room. Then have each group share three things at a time and rotate among the groups. Have someone from each group check off things on their lists that other groups mention. After sharing all of the wonderful successes, ask the group, "What do you think we should do with all of these ideas?" I guarantee someone will say we should put them in the paper!

Well, that is up to you, but you should at least compile the list under the heading of 101 (or 201!) great things about Eastside High School and make this list available to everyone who comes in contact with your school—parents, students, staff, school board members, and central office. Put it on colorful paper and make it an attractive sheet of positive accomplishments. One should also be placed in your Attaboy or Attagirl file (we describe this in Chapter 13).

Not only is this a great experience, it can help set the tone for a goal-setting meeting or just help us put a positive focus on everything we do. It is important to remind ourselves of all of the wonderful things that we accomplish in education.

HALLMARKS OF EXCELLENCE

Hallmarks of Excellence is an activity that can be used with your staff before goal-setting begins, to get everyone in a productive and focused frame of mind. Ask your staff to think of the desired features they want the school to have. These features can relate to the school's mission or vision, to their dreams for the school, or to a current need they have observed. To develop the Hallmarks, have the staff list the features they want to see more of and the features that want to see less of. Using a parallel-column approach requires them to make constructive choices, rather than producing an unrelated grab-bag of features (Glatthorn 1994).

Hallmarks of Excellence can also be used for curriculum design. This allows the teachers to analyze the given subject and identify the desirable features of the curriculum in that field of study. It could also be used as you design global student outcomes, develop mission statements, or draw up student management plans. The applications are endless. The activity allows for focus through open discussion and timely input from the teachers. A sample set of Hallmarks for a school is shown below.

Hallmarks of Excellence for Smith Elementary School

MORE	LESS
1. Respect for others	1. Disrespect for others
2. Writing across the curriculum	2. Writing only occurring in Language Arts time
3. Use of real, quality literature	3. Reliance on the basal text only
4. Problem solving	4. Memorization
5. Opportunities for teacher collaboration	5. Isolated teachers behind closed doors
6. Conflict resolution opportunities for students	6. Punitive approach to all student conflict incidents

PART 2

COMMUNICATION—IT'S WHAT YOU SAY AND HOW YOU SAY IT

5

PERCEPTION—IT'S WHAT YOU SAY AND HOW THEY TOOK IT

Perception is a crucial aspect of leadership. The words you say as a leader are very important, but how people perceive your words is where the rubber really meets the road. What people perceive is what they feel is the truth. Effective leaders understand this aspect of communication and continually try to improve. People do not just want you to hear them; they want to feel that you are really listening to them. Aspects of communication, such as nonverbal communication and listening skills, are essential components of effective leadership. Showing a sincere interest and gaining feedback are also important aspects of the leadership role.

Understanding what people perceive can be difficult. The first thing to understand is that everyone has a different set of "prior experiences" to relate to when communicating. Many new administrators assume that everyone they talk to has had similar experiences and has a similar knowledge base. Because of this, a well-intentioned discussion could end up being very negative. With this in mind, a leader needs to set up communication experiences that are open, honest, and provide for immediate feedback. This provides opportunities for clear communication and ongoing avenues to gain perspective on what people are taking from the conversation. There are many strategies to establish this clear communication process.

LISTENING (THE KEY TO COMMUNICATION)

An initial step in becoming an effective communicator is becoming a better listener. It has been said that the most powerful aspect of communication is listening. This is not just hearing what someone says, but really understanding what that person is saying.

Strategies such as rephrasing what has been said and asking questions about what is said are two ideas to improve listening. "So what you are saying is . . ." and, "What do you mean by . . . ?" are two ways to rephrase and ask questions. Suppose Mr. Johnson, an upset teacher, comes to you about a parent he has just spoken with. Mr. Johnson forcefully says, "I demand not to have Brian in my class because his mother and I can't get along." The first thing you might want to say would be, "Come on now, you know we just can't switch students because you and a parent have issues." But this would not accomplish anything except for Mr. Johnson to be upset with you, while remaining upset with the parent. As an effective communicator, you know that Mr. Johnson has to vent before any solution can be reached.

A better way to address Mr. Johnson would be to say, "What you are telling me is that you are very angry at this parent. How did this situation come about?" This response acknowledges an understanding that Mr. Johnson is upset, and also opens the door for him to vent about how this situation happened. Another response could be, "What do you mean by saying this parent is irrational?" This response shows you are listening, and also allows the teacher an avenue to vent his feelings openly.

After taking the time to listen, you can then look at possible plans of action. One plan I have often used is to show support by offering to be a part of any future meetings with Mr. Johnson and this parent. This plan is twofold; it reinforces your support for Mr. Johnson, and shows the parent that her concerns are important and you want to be a part of any decisions made about her son. When speaking with the mother, I might say, "I am aware of your concerns and would like to know more." Then when meeting with her, I would include in the conversation statements such as "What are some techniques that you use at home to encourage Brian?" "You know Brian better than anyone, so your input is greatly appreciated." "I would appreciate being part of any future meetings that you want to have with Mr. Johnson." "Do you want me to arrange a meeting with the three of us?"

These examples outline two simple listening techniques that will not only improve your understanding of what you are hearing, but also make the person you are talking with *feel* appreciated and listened to. Another great result of utilizing these techniques is that you will listen better, rather than just waiting for your turn to talk.

Listening can also be very powerful in a time of conflict. We all have been in a situation where we felt the person we were speaking with was out of line, expressing ideas or opinions that had no basis. Our natural instinct is to defend ourselves. In this type of emotional situation we tend not to listen, but rather to think of ways to "fire back," to prove that our opponent is wrong. This type of communication is unproductive and very stressful. An effective communicator knows that an upset person has to talk it out first before any type of quality two-way communication can take place. Allowing time for the person to express concerns fully both allows you to get information and allows the upset person to vent.

I experienced one such negative situation in a conference with a teacher and a parent. Knowing that the parent had questions about this teacher, I wanted to be at the conference to support the teacher and try to assist with developing a positive conversation. The parent began, "I can't believe you pick on Hannah like you do!" The teacher responded, "If your daughter would listen in class, I would not have to pick on her!" At that point I could see this conversation was going nowhere. My next step was to become the facilitator. My goal was to support the teacher while providing the parent with an avenue to voice her concern. In such situations, I always remind myself that the most important person is the child, and that parents know and love their children. This helps me to stay objective and not to take comments made under emotional stress personally.

First, I thanked the teacher and the parent for being so concerned about Hannah. I let them know that without their interest and care, this conversation would not be taking place. Then I asked the parent about her concerns. My purpose was to show the mother that we valued her concerns and that we would listen to her. After the mother voiced her concerns, I could see that the teacher was still very upset. At this point, I asked the mother if she had ideas that we could use to help Hannah be successful. This turned the conversation's topic to Hannah, not the teacher. It also focused the conversation on the future, which gets everyone on the same page and sidesteps arguments about actions taken in the past. Now the teacher and parent started to talk about options and solutions for Hannah to be successful. We ended the conversation with a plan of action and a specific avenue of communication for the future.

Such examples demonstrate the tremendous power of listening. Listening brings the conversation to the real issues and past the personality issues. As a leader, be it a department chair, principal, or director of personnel, you can make every situation better by listening. Listening also shows your support for the people you are working with. This is a tremendous avenue to build morale within your organization.

NONVERBAL COMMUNICATION
(IT'S MORE IMPORTANT THAN YOU THINK)

It is clear that nonverbal communication is as important as any other aspect of communication. Being conscious of good eye contact, sitting up, and acknowledging understanding are essential in quality communication. Body language, location relative to the other person, eye contact, and management of interruptions are all crucial aspects of nonverbal communication.

A conversation I once had with a concerned teacher reminds me how strong nonverbal communication can be. She indicated that our counselor did not take her seriously. As we discussed the issue, I learned that the counselor supported the teacher in every way that the teacher asked. When I asked her why she thought the counselor did not take her seriously, she said, "When he talked to me he was sitting behind his desk, leaning back in his chair with his hands behind his head." The counselor had no idea that he was doing this. He was not conscious of the power of nonverbal communication. This example shows that nonverbal communication is very powerful and is a part of every communication encounter.

Being aware of where you are relative to the other person is important. The teacher I just described perceived a negative message not only from the counselor's posture, but from the fact that he was sitting behind the desk. A conversation is likely to feel more comfortable if it does not take place across a barrier such as a desk or a table. Choosing such a barrier-free position expresses your interest and concern and puts you on the same level as the person you are communicating with. In a larger group where there are several people taking part in the conversation, it is very effective to set the chairs up in a circle; this promotes the concept that you are all on the same level and have equal opportunity for input and feedback.

Eye contact is another very important aspect of nonverbal communication. Talking with someone without maintaining eye contact can be very distracting, even insulting! For example, you might continue to work on the computer while visiting with a teacher. You may be listening, but the nonverbal message may be that your computer is more important than the teacher's ideas. Or perhaps, in a hurry to get to a classroom or a meeting, you might keep glancing at the clock during a conversation. Instead of doing this, either stop and really listen or just let the person know you have a meeting and schedule a time to talk later.

The phone can also send a negative nonverbal message. I recall a conversation that I felt was very important. The person I was talking to continued to answer his phone during my visit with him. He indicated to me that he was listening, and maybe he was. But from my perspective, his phone was more important than my concern. I left feeling very upset. Thanks to the invention of voice mail, we can control phone interruptions and not let the phone control us!

The examples described in this section show the importance of nonverbal communication. The nonverbal messages you send can make or break a quality conversation. It is essential not to overlook this crucial aspect of good communication.

SHOWING A SINCERE INTEREST
(THERE IS NO SUBSTITUTE FOR THIS)

As leaders, sometimes we assume that everyone knows we are sincerely interested in the conversation. The people we speak to do not make this assumption. Understanding the personalities and communication styles of the people you work with can help you learn how to show your sincere interest to them. You can never be too interested.

Showing that you are interested comes in many different forms. One way of showing interest is to give people time merely to express their thoughts without immediately working on a solution. Leaders sometimes feel they have to facilitate a solution in every conversation. This is not always true. Many times people just want an ear, not an answer.

As principal, I have had staff come to me with concerns because they needed a sounding board. When I was a middle school principal, for example, a teacher approached me about a teacher on her academic team. She was concerned about problems they were having developing a unit of instruction that would involve the entire team. She went on to say that this teacher was not contributing to the lesson planning with the other team members. After talking to me for a short time, while I simply listened, she came up with her own ideas to address this issue. "What we can do is just set up the plan and then let Cindy know what she can do to help implement it."

This conversation reinforced to me that sometimes being an open ear not only shows that you're interested, but also provides a sounding board for people to think aloud. With this approach, you can often allow the other person to keep the responsibility for determining a solution.

Some teachers may feel your interest is shown through follow-up and providing solutions. In some situations, one conversation is only the start of the process of showing sincere interest. Follow-up and providing solutions should take place in these situations. An example of follow-up is handling a discipline situation. The initial conversation may be a referral note from a teacher about a student disrupting the class. In this situation the first step is to visit with the teacher about the concern. I recommend doing this in person in the classroom. Going to the classroom right away, or soon after the referral is sent, is best. Even if the teacher is in the middle of a lesson you can make sure he sees you, and you can leave a quick note about seeing him at a time that does not interrupt his class. Even though you did not visit with the teacher right away, you showed him your interest and support by wanting to take immediate steps to help the situation.

The next step is to actually discuss the situation with the teacher. This can give you insight, not only about what happened, but about how the teacher is feeling about the situation. Knowing how the teacher feels is very important. I handle the incident differently based on the teacher's response. If the teacher is very upset and frustrated, I will focus on eliminating that frustration with my actions. If the teacher says something like "Tim will be fine, he just needed a time-out," I will handle it differently. The important thing to remember is that both of these reactions could arise from the same student behavior.

Let's say the student, Tim, slammed his book shut and refused to do the assignment. If the teacher is very upset, I would meet with Tim and his parents about the importance of doing his work and draw out future consequences, positive and negative. I would say something like, "For the best interest of Tim being successful at school, and not isolated from the rest of the class, he really needs to be a positive part of the class." I would personalize it with Tim and his parents based on their interest and ideas about the situation. If Tim feels athletics is important, I might be specific on how doing his work affects his eligibility to play. If Tim hates the class, I would remind him that the more he does in class means the less he does outside of the class, which means the less time he has to think about it. Obviously these conversations also depend on Tim's age, but personalizing it is the key at any age.

Now that I have spoken to the student and the student's parents, I would follow up with the teacher on next steps. Remember that the teacher was very frustrated and upset. I would first and foremost visit *in person*. E-mail is fine for distributing announcements and memos, but is not recommended for good follow-up. Writing cannot show things like emotion and eye contact and cannot respond to feelings about the news. I would inform this teacher that I visited with Tim and his parents and let them know the seriousness of Tim's disrupting the class and refusing to work. I would go on to say that Tim and his parents know that if this continues they will need to come to school to discuss this again. This lets the teacher know that I recognize his concerns and want to show support for him. In this situation, as always, focusing on what is best for the student and focusing on the future are the keys. By the end of this incident, the teacher not only is feeling supported, but has a mindset of what interventions he can try next time so that neither Tim nor he gets so frustrated.

Now let's talk about the same situation when the teacher is not overly concerned and just wanted Tim to have a time-out. Again, I would follow up in person. I would acknowledge the teacher for being so patient and proactive about Tim's frustration. I would explain to the teacher that I contacted the parents and reinforced with them the fact that the teacher is doing everything he can to accommodate Tim's frustrations, but if Tim's actions continue, I will have to intervene. This not only shows the teacher my appreciation, but sets *me* up to be the "bad guy" if the conduct continues. My hope is that these actions encourage the teacher to continue to try alternative strategies to help Tim be successful, knowing that I will back him up or step in, if necessary.

Still another way of showing interest is to ask about the idea or concern at a later time. Too many times, leaders overlook the follow-up, and it does not get done. I have found that following up later through a note, a question, or just a "How is everything going?" comment proves to the teacher that you remembered his dilemma. In this case with the student, Tim, I would definitely ask how he was doing at a later time.

The examples just talked about are "win-win" strategies; the final result is positive for all involved. No matter what the interest level or the communication style you have with the people you work with, taking time to show support for them *always* pays big dividends.

FEEDBACK (THE BREAKFAST OF CHAMPIONS)

Obtaining and responding to staff feedback is an essential part of the communication process when improving staff morale. Gaining knowledge through feedback comes in many forms. The point of any form of feedback is to be conscious of it and take appropriate action. If you ask for feedback, and your staff provides it, you need to make sure you respond to this feedback. Here are some avenues for feedback:

1. One-to-one conversations
   a. in hallways
   b. before and after school
   c. during teacher planning time
2. Informal day-to-day conversations
   a. during duty time (cafeteria, hallway, playground)
   b. before and after meetings
3. Grade-level/department meetings
   a. questions about support staff
   b. ideas to assist you to be supportive
4. Staff meetings
   a. have discussions about building-wide activities
   b. share thoughts about district meetings and their impact at the building level
5. Various committee meetings (budget, literacy, and social)
   a. visit about previous procedures and how to address issues
   b. provide information that was asked for at previous meetings
6. End-of-year principal survey
   a. distribute towards the end of the year
   b. collect before the teachers are finished for the summer
   c. compile and distribute results in a summer letter
   d. discuss ways to address issues at the beginning of the next year

As indicated above, collecting feedback is just the first step. What you do with this information is the key that drives great communication. As a new principal in a building of veteran teachers, I ran staff meetings much as they were run in the past. It seemed that everyone was happy with them. At the end of the year I handed out a principal evaluation survey. As I read through the comments, I found that the teachers wanted staff meetings to be more reflective, rather than geared toward delivery of information. This was very enlightening. I, too, wanted the meetings to be more reflective. This was a reminder to me that you never have too much feedback.

Now, I compile all of the suggestions (excluding positive comments towards me and comments that are private) and give the list back to the teachers. This allows the teachers to see that I am being honest and open with each of these concerns, and shows how the ideas are being addressed. This sets the table for open discussions in all aspects of school improvement.

The reason I do not compile comments like "You're doing great" or "Your support for teachers is nice" is that although they are reinforcement for me, they are not avenues for improving communication. Furthermore, general statements are tough to use. I focus on specific ways to improve support. This is to model that it is OK to look at how to improve. Improving does not mean things are bad, it just means we can always get better. This helps staff become comfortable with quality communication that sometimes includes constructive criticism.

Here are examples of ways to respond to feedback:

Follow-up conversations. These conversations can happen directly after an incident, at the end of the day, or the next day. I try not to let them wait too long. Examples of how to start these conversations are: "How is everything going with…?" "How can I help with what we talked about?" or a simple, "Please let me know if I can do anything else. Thanks."

Notes/memos/e-mail. As with follow-up conversations, these need to be written in a timely manner. I also try to use these as reinforcement. Examples of these written notes may include: "Thanks for taking the time to set up such an effective plan." "Please let me know if I can assist in any way." "Thanks for being so positive with Mrs. Smith! I know it was not the most comfortable situation. Please let me know if I can help in any way." or, "Great job today in the staff meeting! When you have time please let me know how you felt it went, and how I can support you in the future." These are just a few of examples of what to say. The premise of any written message is to offer support, as well as provide an open avenue for follow-up conversations.

Compiling and discussing suggestions from surveys. My end-of-the-year survey is directed toward finding out ideas, suggestions, and concerns about all aspects of our school. The survey includes questions about principal support, staff meetings, grade-level meetings, schedule, duty plans, library support, technology ideas, and professional growth. If teachers take the time to fill this out, I feel I should do something constructive with it. I compile the specific ideas and concerns into a letter I send them over the summer. Then we discuss these ideas at the first staff meeting of the next year. From this start, we, as a group, make decisions and plans based on this input.

Making adjustments based on people's suggestions. Involve the staff when making decisions and plans based on their suggestions. This builds trust and "buy-in." An example is to form a committee of interested teachers to examine the professional development budget and build a plan based on teachers' suggestions. This shows trust by working directly with the budget and promotes "buy-in" because the professional development ideas are not coming from an outside source, but are coming from within the staff.

Not responding at all. I do not advise this. In some situations, because of time constraints or other priorities, responding to feedback does not happen. What we need to realize is that no response is still a response. No response still sends a strong message: "Your feedback is not important enough to address." I am in no way saying that we, as leaders, need to respond to and solve every complaint. I know trying to do that would drive me crazy! What I am saying is that some type of acknowledgment needs to be made to support the staff that cares enough to give you feedback.

There are many ways to improve the perception of how your staff sees you. A few years ago I worked with a principal who was well respected by everyone who worked with him. His staff's perception of him was that he was honest, hardworking, and above all, that he respected his teachers. He expressed two guidelines for principals:

1. **Never take credit.**
2. **Always support teachers in public.**

Not taking credit can take many forms. You might acknowledge in public (for example, at a PTA meeting) the grants written by your staff, even though you may have done most of the writing. When the superintendent acknowledges improved discipline because of a new program you implemented, respond with, "The teachers have worked so hard to make this happen." Finally, something as simple as referring to your school as "our school," not "my school" is important.

There are also many ways to support teachers in public. You can thank the teachers at an assembly for their hard work. You can let the PTA know how much the teachers did to develop and plan a professional development day and how it will impact their kids in a positive way. You can even have everyone give a round of applause to the custodians for having such a great-looking building for open house night. Remembering these two suggestions has been very helpful to me throughout my career.

Having an accurate perspective on how the people you work with are receiving your thoughts and ideas is paramount for quality leadership to take place. The examples outlined in this chapter—listening, nonverbal communication, showing a sincere interest, and getting feedback—are simple but effective ways to improve your knowledge of how your staff is perceiving you. As an educational leader, the better your understanding of this perception, the higher the morale. A final thought about perception is *never assume anything!* You can never be too aware of how people perceive you.

6

THE FRIDAY FOCUS— A STAFF MEMO THAT WORKS!

One concept that has been much discussed in the literature regarding effective leaders is the idea of leadership versus management. This debate often centers around that idea that "management" is old hat and unrelated to being a good leader. In other words, organizational skills, pushing paper, being able to handle finances, and so forth were appropriate a few decades ago, but are no longer valued. Instead, the desire now is to have someone who can provide "leadership"—i.e. a visionary, a relationship builder, a communicator. We feel though, that it is not an "either or." Instead, the need is to have both.

One tool that can support both of these efforts is to have a staff memo which can provide management *and* leadership. Management is always important in order to have high morale in an organization. It may not be enough in and of itself, but it is an essential part. Think of the management element of an educational leader in comparison to the classroom management skills of a teacher. Just as a teacher with classroom management skills may not be an effective teacher, a principal with good management skills still may not be an effective leader. However, a principal without good management skills, just like a teacher without classroom management skills, will *never* be effective.

A staff memo, if it is developed and used properly, can help provide both management and leadership for an organization. If both of these can be in place, then the morale of the staff is much more likely to be positive and productive. Without a tool that is widely distributed to all staff on a regular basis, an educational leader is missing an excellent opportunity to dramatically impact morale. If done correctly, the staff memo can be *the* most important resource for a principal in both managing and leading a school. It can be informational, organizational, and inspirational at the same time. Let's take a look at one model called the Friday Focus.

FRIDAY FOCUS—DEVELOPING A STAFF MEMO THAT WORKS

One important facet of effectively motivating any and all faculty and staff is having appropriate vehicles to be able to do so. In a study of over 300 elementary schools in Indiana, Whitaker (1997) identified four schools with "more effective" climates and four schools with "less effective" climates. Teachers at each of these schools were asked to complete an instrument describing the climate of their school. On-site visits and interviews with teachers and the principals revealed several key differences between the principals of the more effective and the less effective schools. One of the differences between these two groups was that the more effective principals have regular, positive, weekly memos for their faculty and staff. None of the less effective principals produced positive faculty memos on a regular basis.

As we discussed in Chapter 4, knowing the impact that the principal has on a school, it is crucial that principals firmly establish their own personal beliefs and work to effect an appropriate belief system throughout the school. One of the most important and easiest ways to do this is with a weekly memo for the staff. Though it may also be of value to have an additional memo for the students, parents, and others, we are going to focus on the development of a memo for *all staff*—teachers, cooks, custodians, bus drivers, everyone who works at the school. If the staff memo is done properly, it may not be appropriate to share with other groups such as students and parents.

THE HISTORY OF THE FRIDAY FOCUS

I was 25 years old when I took my first principalship. I remember walking down the hall early in the school year. A teacher stopped me and asked, "Are you ready for the big assembly this afternoon?" When I finally realized that *I was the principal* and she was speaking to me, I muttered (quite unconvincingly, I am sure), "Yep, I'm ready."

Then I scurried into the office and asked my wonderful secretary, "Do we have an assembly today?" When she responded affirmatively, I raced around, found the custodian, and worked out all of the bleacher arrangements, equipment needs, and the like. When it was time for the assembly, I got on the intercom and interrupted every class with an announcement regarding the dismissal time and other logistics for the assembly. Teachers were unhappy about the interruption; some were even caught off guard by the late notice. Definitely, it was not a positive event for staff morale! Though disaster was averted—sort of—I vowed that there had to be a better way of doing things.

This scene was replayed several times in different ways during my first year as a principal. I would go home, share my tales of woe with my wife, and wonder what I could do differently. My wife, who was a teacher in a different school, suggested something that seemed to help everyone get organized. Once a week, her principal put a little half-page memo in their mailboxes, giving a schedule for the upcoming week. Every once in a while, he included a quote or comment that was inspirational, funny, or motivational. This helped the teachers stay informed. More importantly, I saw that something like this would help me stay up to date. So, somewhat reluctantly, I gave it a shot.

THINKING THROUGH THE LOGISTICS

One of my first questions was When do I do it? Is there any advantage to certain days of the week? Another early question was Who should receive it?

The timing of the Friday Focus was essential in terms of morale. When I examined when there seemed to be the highest percentage of discipline referrals by day of the week, the overwhelming winner was Friday. And, it makes sense. The teachers are tired, the students are wound up, and everyone is just a little bit more impatient. The result was that more students were sent to the office for discipline. Well, I am a big believer in working smarter, not harder. So I thought, if one of the goals of this memo is to help the morale of the staff (and thus help my morale with fewer disciplinary referrals!) then I might as well have it available on Friday morning. Thus, each Thursday before I left work, I would run off copies of the Friday Focus. I put one in each staff member's mailbox, so that the first thing people would see when they arrived on Friday morning was the Friday Focus. This would assist in setting the tone for the school on the day when everyone may be the most tired.

GETTING ORGANIZED

Having the memo in mailboxes by Friday morning also allowed the organization of our school to increase. Because it included a calendar for the next week, the memo could help teachers plan accordingly. I also discovered that typing out next week's calendar on my computer caused me to organize my own thoughts. It also gave me the chance to think through the organizational details of events such as assemblies or field trips. Communicating any schedule changes or logistical operations allowed the entire school to be on the same page. All teachers dislike having their routine disrupted, but they despise having this happen with little or no notice.

Developing and distributing a calendar on a regular basis helped the entire school be more organized. Eventually, I included a two-week calendar with each Friday Focus. This allowed for an increased level of planning and organization both for me and for the staff. Each week, the calendar was updated as necessary and issued for the coming week, with a new calendar for the second week.

The other aspect of organization that was so critical was to be able to provide information regarding upcoming schedule changes due to a special event. Additionally, I could provide information regarding dismissal times, seating arrangements, and special info regarding upcoming assemblies, field trips, and the like. By including this in the Friday Focus at least four things occurred:

1. Everyone in the school became aware of events that might change their schedules.
2. Every staff member had *written* directions for upcoming special events.
3. We did not have to spend valuable time during staff meetings on logistical events. (Any organizational things that can be done in the form of a memo should be done that way. Staff meeting time is way too valuable to waste on information that can be handled more efficiently.)
4. Everyone involved had an opportunity to think through the logistics of an upcoming event in advance so that any necessary changes to the schedule could occur with as much notice as possible. For instance, the staff could look at the altered schedule for the assembly next week and let me know of any problems with the timing or logistics. Then if it was essential that we change the arrangements, we could do it with plenty of notice. This allowed me to be second-guessed in advance! Then, I could actually do something about it.

Here is an example of a logistical reminder from a Friday Focus. I was principal of a new school and this was our very first all-school assembly:

Our assembly with the Kansas City Royals baseball players is now scheduled for 2:20 on Wednesday the 19th. We will have all students come down to the gym and get seated at 2:15 and sit with their teams in the gym. We will have 7th grade sit on the right side bleachers, 6th grade on the left side (looking out from the stage), and 8th grade will sit in folding chairs. The baseball players will visit with the students and then answer questions from the audience if time allows. We will dismiss students for the day from the gymnasium. Let's escort 6th grade students to their Blazer Time classes from their 7th period class at 2:10. In other words, let's hang on to our 7th hour students on Wednesday for 10 extra minutes and then 8th period classes will not have to meet for just 10 minutes. Please make sure we bring our students down at 2:15 and that we use discretion to sit by and/or between any students that may particularly enjoy conversing. Thanks, and let me know if this makes sense.

This is an example of something that I would put in the Friday Focus two weeks in advance. That way there would be plenty of time for feedback if someone else foresaw any problems. With a complicated item like this, I would also include the information in next week's Focus, so it would be fresh in the minds of staff members. Much information is not that complicated, but if people already know what to do, they do not have to read the information. However, teachers generally love as much direction as possible and this way the entire school can be on the same page.

A STAFF DEVELOPMENT TOOL

The weekly memo should also be used as a staff development tool, as well as a method to consistently keep the beliefs of the principal in front of the staff. Attaching articles, inserting paragraphs about personal beliefs, and the like are important ways to accomplish this. Stronge (1990) felt that one essential role of a principal is to communicate the goals of the school with the faculty; and this method of correspondence will enable this to occur on a regular basis. This can help promote growth and direction for all staff.

There are many ways to accomplish these things. One of our favorites is to attach an article to the Friday Focus and then summarize one or two of the main points in the memo itself. An example:

I have included a copy of a letter to the editor from *Language Arts* magazine with this week's Friday Focus. It is a neat reflection by a teacher as she grows into using literature sets with her students, loves it, and begins to realize what a lifelong learner she wants to become.

This approach accomplishes several things. The leader reminds everyone in the school about literature sets in a way that is positive. People do not even have to read the letter to get the gist of it because of the summary in the Focus. It also allows someone else's view to be shared with the staff. A regular memo is a natural resource that makes the flow of staff development much more integrated into the school and into the role of the leader.

Another way to use the Friday Focus for staff development and growth is what I call "seed planting." As leaders, we know that if we can get someone else to come up with the idea instead of us, then it is more likely to be adopted. As Dwight D. Eisenhower once said, "Leadership is the art of getting other people to do things you want to do, because they want to do them." The Friday Focus can be of tremendous assistance in this area. I liked to use statements such as:

I happened to be in someone's classroom the other day and I saw the most wonderful Cooperative Learning activity taking place. The students were so engaged in . . .

Let's examine what just happened with this statement. Teachers who use cooperative learning feel reinforced and probably think I was talking about them! Teachers who have never heard of cooperative learning now at least have a seed planted regarding the terminology. My staff is reminded of my positive view of cooperative learning. I present cooperative learning in a positive light to all staff members.

A similar approach can be used regarding things that no one in your building is currently using, but that you would like teachers in your school to consider. Let's look at another approach on the topic of cooperative learning if no teacher in your school is currently using it. In your Friday Focus you might write:

> I saw something neat at a school I was visiting the other day. I happened to be in the classroom of this dynamic teacher and she was using something she called "cooperative learning." The students in her classroom were so excited and engaged in learning. Wow! Are any of you familiar with this approach? I'd love to learn more about it.

This is a way to introduce a new idea or concept to your school in a way that is likely to be accepted by your staff. Think about which teachers are most likely to be intrigued. Your superstars, of course. Any idea that they think is beneficial to students will attract their attention. Then, if they decide to learn more about it and eventually try it in their classrooms, you now have something to build on in your school. Plus, if a superstar tries a new idea, it is likely to work well.

If you do not have any takers with this first mention, you could a couple of weeks later attach an article and write something like this:

> Remember a couple of weeks ago when I mentioned seeing someone using a fantastic concept called "cooperative learning"? Well, I happened to find an article on the topic that I thought you might find of interest. It mentions that . . .

This way the article is much more natural and you are presenting it as a service to the faculty. You can also add things like "a couple of you were asking about . . . ." or "an article that one of you shared with me," or "some of us were chatting the other day about . . . ." Phrases like this imply that peers were involved in the idea and this can be very beneficial. This is what Covey (1989) refers to as "expanding your circle of influence."

THE CIRCLE OF INFLUENCE

The Friday Focus is a tremendous tool for expanding the circle of influence of the principal. If you recall, in Chapter 2 we described the process of attempting to have teachers make their rooms more visually attractive. We described how three super-star teachers were at a meeting in another school, saw how appealing the rooms were in that other school, and then decorated their rooms in very attractive manner. We also mentioned that we wrote in the Friday Focus:

> Has anybody been in Mary's, Nancy's, or Jackie's rooms lately? Wow! No wonder the kids love their classes. When I went into their classrooms I wanted to bring a sleeping bag and stay all night!

This was an example of using the respect that others hold to expand your influence. If I had not had a staff memo to brag about these classrooms, it is likely that the only rooms to be improved would have been those of the three superstar teachers. Instead, because everyone could read how great those rooms looked, everyone's interest was raised. The impact on the school was greater and much more immediate with the Friday Focus as a communication resource.

There are two other primary ways to expand your circle of influence using the Friday Focus: by quoting others in the Friday Focus, and by sending the Friday Focus to those you want to influence.

One of my favorite things to do in the Friday Focus was to quote others. Sometimes I would use names, but more often I would use anonymous quotes. They might be from parents, students, visitors, or others, and I would describe the source in general terms. I want to share a couple of examples.

Each week at the bottom of the Friday Focus I would have a thought for the week. These might include quotes by famous people, funny sayings, or inspirational comments. They also often included comments by unidentified students and parents. As you know, we are big believers in the appearance of a school. A way to reinforce teachers who have attractive classrooms and encourage others is by quoting a third party:

> "I cannot believe all of the decorations in your school. How do your teachers do it? I bet the kids love it here!"—a visitor at Eastside Elementary.

By quoting a "real person," the comment may even be more influential than if you quote yourself. You have reinforced every teacher who has attempted to decorate, you have encouraged others to improve the appearance of their areas, and you did it in an anonymous public fashion. That way everyone hears it, but no one is resentful of others. It also avoids the challenge of trying to publicly reinforce people and yet being afraid you will leave someone out.

I want to share another example of using anonymous quotes to expand your circle of influence and positively affect morale. At one school where I became principal, the previous administration had a legacy of "kick butt and take names" as their approach to discipline. Yelling, sarcasm, and even paddling were their discipline tools of choice. Not only do I disagree with this approach, I find it offensive. However, because of the length of tenure of the previous administration, the teachers in the school felt that this is what "discipline" was all about.

Well, I had to establish my own style and approach to student management. I believe that we always treat every student with dignity. My goal with students and parents when I suspended a student was to have them say "Thank you" at the end of our conference. As most of you know, we actually can accomplish this with the correct approach.

Anyhow, my concern was how the teachers would make the transition to a more humanistic approach to the way students are treated. I was concerned that they might not feel supported—and we all know that making sure teachers feel supported is at least as important as simply supporting them.

One area that is always important in a school is the cafeteria. Student behavior in the cafeteria is always a challenge, and yet it is a critical element in establishing behavior expectations in the school. Well, about three weeks into the school year a well-respected teacher came to me and said, "The staff is concerned about discipline in the school. They are not sure the approach by the administrators is effective."

I asked her what she meant, since she had not referred any students to the office and those teachers that had done so seemed very satisfied. She said that she had heard teachers complaining about the behavior of students in the lunchroom and that there was a growing concern regarding the principal's and assistant principal's ability to control the students.

Of course, my first reaction was to question myself. "Am I too weak? Should I be 'meaner'?" But as I reflected, I realized that the challenge here was much greater than the behavior of the students. I realized that no teachers ever even entered the cafeteria—only the administrators were there. Thus even if the assistant principal and I were to attempt to "crack down" on the students, no one would ever know. What a dilemma. Furthermore, we thought that things were going really well, and so did the cafeteria workers. But we could never prove this, because no one else ever observed the lunchroom. On the other hand, if the level of concern continued to rise among the teachers, we would lose credibility regardless of how things were actually going. It was a *perception* we were battling, not a reality.

Thus, we needed to create a perception that all was well and communicate it to the teachers. Friday Focus to the rescue! Fortunately, our school hosted many visitors, as we had quite a few programs, teachers, and innovations that others wanted to see. Often, I would use these outsiders to expand my circle of influence with the faculty. Perspective is a very powerful influence. A couple of weeks later we had some visitors from a wealthy district, one that was highly regarded throughout the state.

After their visit, in my Friday Focus I wrote:

> Our visitors from Smithton spoke very highly of everyone's enthusiasm at school. They were so complimentary of our faculty. They also commented on how well-behaved our students were. Sometimes it is helpful to gets an outsider's perspective. They even wondered what we put in the kids' lunches to get them to be so well-behaved in the cafeteria. It was nice to hear that.

Amazingly, starting that Friday, I had several teachers come up and say how much better the students were behaving in the lunchroom. They commented that they had heard that things were really going well in the cafeteria. Looking back, I know that we did not change one thing we were doing. However, the staff got a psychological boost because we expanded our circle of influence.

Other quotes from parents and students included things like

♦ "Your teachers are nice—you are really lucky"—a mom was overheard to say at open house night.

♦ "Can I nominate my teacher for teacher of the week?"— a student of the week asked.

♦ "Wow! I hear great things about your school!"—a community leader stopped me at the grocery store.

Obviously, everyone in the school feels that they are that anonymous child's teacher, that the mom is talking about them, and so on. You also reinforce being nice, promoting your school, and making positive impressions with parents. Without a tool like the Friday Focus to expand your circle of influence, it would be almost impossible to have this powerful impact.

Another factor in expanding your circle of influence is deciding who should receive the Friday Focus. The list includes all teachers, cooks, custodians, and others inside your school; in addition, sending it on a weekly basis to important people outside of your school is a very powerful way to put your school in a positive light with others.

We would recommend sending your weekly memo to the principals of all of the other schools in your district and to the superintendent and all other central office people. You might also consider your PTA president, business partner, and so on, but we feel that other principals and the central office staff are essential. Let's take a look at the reasoning behind this.

First of all, what kind of information goes into the Friday Focus? Positive news. Never negative information. As people read each week about all of the great things taking place in your school, how does this influence their view of your school and your leadership? Just think about the comment regarding the behavior of the students in the cafeteria or the parents mentioning how nice the teachers are. Do you think the superintendent likes to hear this kind of news? Of course. And, more importantly, you *want* the superintendent and other administrators to hear this kind of news. Well, you could call them and tell them—

but we know how much everybody likes those who "toot their own horn." The Friday Focus allows you to "brag without bragging." You did not say how well-behaved the students were; someone else did. You did not comment on how nicely decorated your school is; a visitor did. The people you quote have more credibility than you do, and yet if you don't write the positive comments up in the Friday Focus and then distribute it, nobody but you would know about them.

And when you specifically mention someone's name, then the principals at the other schools and the central office people learn about that person's accomplishment and have an opportunity to share their congratulations. As you add to the list of those receiving the weekly memo, mentioning a person by name can expand your circle of influence in still other important ways.

Let's say your district's business manager, Mr. Jones, is not particularly well regarded. And let's say that generally the only thing the business manager hears is complaints; after all, there is never quite enough money. However, one week you write this:

> I was feeling sorry for myself the other day, as we all do sometimes, and then I thought about our business manager, Mr. Jones. I thought to myself, bless his heart. Each year he does everything he can to provide us with every possible resource and yet all he ever hears is complaints about not enough money. Well, I have decided that from now on I am going to be thankful for everything Mr. Jones does for us. Without his leadership we would not be able to have all of the resources that we do. The next time I see him I am going to thank him for all of his efforts—and if you have a chance, it might be nice if we all did the same.

Well, I know that one person who always receives the Friday Focus is—you guessed it—the business manager, Mr. Jones. And he knows that his boss reads it and so do all of the other principals in the district. Do you think Mr. Jones is glad I wrote that? Of course he is. Think about what that does for Mr. Jones' perspective. More importantly, think about what that does for Mr. Jones' perspective of you.

What might happen if a couple of weeks later you wrote in the Friday Focus:

> Does anyone know where we can get any additional resources so that we can put six additional computers in the lab? Our enrollment has gone up, and we now have up to six students in our classes who do not have access to a work station. If you know of a business who might donate, a parent who might assist, or if you think we ought to have a giant garage sale, please let me know. I hate to see our students suffer because of this shortage.

There is a chance that Mr. Jones may call you up and say that he found some funds that you can use to acquire those computers. Maybe not, but what do you have to lose? It worked for us!

FOCUSING ON MORALE

The Friday Focus is an excellent motivational tool. It should be used to mention good things about the school. Examples include everything from "When I was in Mrs. Johnson's room I was so impressed with…" to "I asked four students in the cafeteria on Wednesday what they liked best about school and they said, 'The way the teachers treat us!'" We have given several examples of this approach. Additionally, it should be used for more direct praise and tone-setting.

Let's take a look at a way to reinforce teachers for their efforts on open house night *and* brag about your attendance for the benefit of central office staff members who receive the weekly memo:

> Thanks so much for all of your efforts on Open House Night! We had a great turnout, the hot dogs were excellent, and best of all, we had a chance to really show off. Estimates are around 1,500 people attended. All I heard was how much everyone's kids like the school because of the teachers. It's funny—our facility is so beautiful, you would think that is what we would hear about, but instead it's "my son sure loves his teachers" or "my

daughter can't wait to get to school and go to her classes." Thanks to each of you for making last night a success and for making each day a success for our students. Great job!

The tone is set for a great Friday at school!

Emotional periods like the holidays are a wonderful opportunity to provide a positive perspective for a faculty. Here is part of a December 22nd Friday Focus:

Holidays are such a nice time to reflect on our lives, to evaluate if we are the kind of person that we want to be, and also to give thanks for all of life's many blessings. Well, I know that for myself and for the students here, each of you provides many hours and days that we can all be thankful for and will look back on with fond memories. Thanks to each one of you for choosing education and making a difference in the lives of the students at Connor Middle School. Have a joyful holiday and please remember to take care of your family and yourselves. Thanks for being you.

How does this make you feel? What kind of a tone does it set with the staff? You can also accomplish the same effect with humor. That same Friday Focus could conclude with

Thought for the week—"I'm gonna miss Connor School over the vacation!"—overhead in the lunchroom (from a student, not a teacher).

The Friday Focus does not preclude other efforts. It is still important to write personal notes and praise in person. But a positive weekly staff memo does provide a vehicle to help affect the morale of everyone in the school. It can consistently help set a tone which will infiltrate into the classrooms and be the voice of the school. It can have an effect that provides both breadth and depth in a way that no other avenues provide.

If a principal gets in a routine of having these informative, uplifting, and belief-focusing memos, the teachers will look forward to it each Friday morning and it will play a critical role in establishing and communicating the school-wide belief system. Setting a positive tone for the school is a very important way to help build the morale of everyone in the school.

FEEL FREE TO LEAVE AT 3:05 . . . HAVE A GREAT WEEKEND

I concluded every Friday Focus with the comment, "Feel free to leave at 3:05 today, and have a great weekend." This definitely had an important and positive effect on the morale in my school, for two reasons.

The first is pretty obvious. Teachers were required to stay at school until 3:30 each day. However, ending the week with the opportunity to leave at 3:05 helped to set a positive tone each Friday morning. Most teachers stayed later than 3:30 every Friday, but somehow it made them feel better just knowing they could leave. In addition, staff members who were going away for the weekend or had just survived "the week that wouldn't end!" were welcome to take off at 3:05 on Friday afternoon. I always assumed that anyone who was sitting around on a Friday afternoon, staring at the clock, waiting for 3:30 to arrive, was probably not very productive anyhow.

The other reason that I closed the Friday Focus with this comment may not be as obvious. Before I became the principal, teachers that were less student-centered were "sneaking out" of school before 3:30 on Friday afternoons. The problem wasn't that they were leaving—the problem was that the most productive staff members were upset because others were breaking the rules!

Well, as a leader, I had two choices. I could wait out in the parking lot on Friday afternoons, hoping to "catch" these sneaks. Or, I could change the "rule" so that they did not have to sneak. My concern, of course, was not to relieve the guilty consciences of those teachers who were violating a rule. My goal was to help the more positive teachers not be upset with others whom they saw as shirking their professional obligations. So, my solution was to let everyone go early on Friday.

Interestingly, the actual work schedules on Fridays did not change. My hardest-working staff members worked well into the late afternoon and the other staff left shortly after three o'clock. However, the valuable result of my "feel free to leave" was that my most positive teachers were no longer upset. Because it was no longer a rule, no one was breaking it anymore!

GENERAL TIPS AND GUIDELINES

Here are some guidelines that may be beneficial as you develop your own Friday Focus.

Create an attractive format that is used weekly. Select a format that looks very readable and appealing. See Figure 3 for an example of the basic format for the front of the Friday Focus. The other side of the page features a two-week calendar of upcoming events.

Use colored paper. Choose a color at the start of the year, use this color for the Friday Focus each week, and do not use paper of this color for anything else in the school. Make it truly special. You may be tempted to send the Friday Focus on e-mail, but we would advise against that; it is much more likely to be lost in the shuffle. As you consistently set a positive tone in your memos, you may well discover that almost all of your staff will save each copy. So, splurge and make them unique.

Make sure it is in staff mailboxes at the same time each week. Whether you choose Friday, Monday, or some other time during the week, be consistent. People will look forward to and expect your memo.

Post the current Friday Focus in the teacher's lounge. This can allow for quick reference for those who misplace theirs. It may even help set a positive tone in the lounge.

Collect quotes, inspirational thoughts, and cartoons. You will find that this becomes an easy habit. If you accumulate a stash of quotes, you can use them as appropriate without having to scramble around at the last minute for your weekly thought. You will find that others will start to contribute good ones as well.

Make notes of events you see when you are "out and about." This can come in handy when you are writing your Focus. The more personal the items, the better.

In your planner, keep a running list of items that you want to include each week. Jot down notes to yourself throughout the week and you will find that finishing up on Thursday is

---

FIGURE 3

Eastside Middle School
Friday Focus
September 10th

1. Thanks so much for all of your efforts on Open House Night! We had a great turnout, the hot dogs were excellent, and best of all we had a chance to really show off. Estimates are around 1,500 people. All I heard was how much everyone's kids like the school because of the teachers. It's funny, because of our beautiful facility you would think that is what we would hear about, but instead its "my son sure loves his teachers or my daughter can't wait to get to school and go to her classes." Thanks to each of you for making last night a success and for making each day a success for our students. Great job!

2. Congratulations to Beth Myers, Donna Houseman, and Scott Culp, our three faculty council representatives!

3. I spent a couple of hours last night with a strategic planning committee from the Marshall Public Schools (our neighbors to the south!). This committee was comprised of community members, teachers, administrators, and students. I gave them a tour of the building and discussed our various programs with them. They wanted me to extend to you their congratulations on our Outstanding Schools Award, but they also wanted me to share how impressed they were with our curricular focus, teaching practices, and school climate. They chose our building because they wanted to take a look at "what's right with education."

4. I also really meant what I said in the note on Tuesday about how important it is for all of us to focus on our successes and we have so many here! Over and over everyone I talk to - students, parents, and community members all say how great things are here at Eastside and the adults consistently share that their children come home excited and challenged by school. Yesterday morning I had a meeting with some community business members and they went on and on about all of the great things they have heard about us and what a shot in the arm it is for our community and students. We are doing what we hoped to and let's make sure we enjoy it. Way to go gang!

5. Happy Friday to everyone! Congratulations on making it through our first full week of school! I hope each of you has the chance to recharge this weekend. You should really be proud of the what you have accomplished. I know I am proud of you!

6. Feel free to leave at 3:05 today. Have a great fall weekend! P.S. every Friday is staff T-shirt day - be there, be square (or be like me and be both!)

Thought for the week, "Your teachers are really nice, you're lucky" Overheard a mom talking to her daughter at open house night.

simple. You might also just keep the weekly memo as a file on your computer all the time, so that you can develop it throughout the week.

Include "Friday Focus Featured Folks." Featuring one or two staff members each week can help promote the dynamics of the building. Rather than writing them all yourself, ask each staff member to write a couple of paragraphs of self-description and turn it in to the secretary. Assign everyone a specific due date at the start of the year to spread out the contributions. Start off with a couple of good writers, to establish the tone you want to set. People will be amazed at how much they discover about others whom they have worked with for years.

Offer your "quote of the week." You have seen the many uses for this.

Make sure you are upbeat and comfortable when you write. If you want to set a positive tone, it helps to be in that frame of mind. It is essential to maintain a consistently upbeat feel to the memo so that you can establish the perspective you desire.

Put your heart into it and *have fun!* The Friday Focus was our single most valuable tool as school leaders. When we first started developing them, we had others read through each edition to make sure that it set the tone we wanted. We also had staff members proofread for grammar and spelling. Once you are comfortable with your own Friday Focus, you will find that it sets a great tone for you. It is a consistent reminder of all of the great things that are taking place in your school every week.

7

MAKING A DIFFERENCE EACH DAY

The daily actions of the school leader play an integral role in staff morale. The decisions we make, the words we say and write, and the smiles we share (or don't share) all have the power to improve morale or slowly destroy it. How often you choose to make yourself visible to your staff can also affect morale. I reminisce back to two of my experiences as a teacher. One involved working with a principal who rarely emerged from his office and was a foreigner in my classroom. When he would finally come to observe me, I experienced an odd feeling. I wanted him to see the exciting things I did with my students, but the whole time he was there it wasn't natural or comfortable. My students had the same reaction; they became awkward and stilted in their responses to my teaching strategies. On a day when I wanted to shine, the children and I became clumsy and uncomfortable in our quest for learning.

I contrast this with the principal who was in my room regularly. He knew my students and interacted frequently with us in our classroom learning community. He appeared each day at our door and became a part of our lessons. Sometimes he just quietly observed, while other times he became a part of our activity. This visit might last anywhere from three to thirty minutes. His presence was never an intrusion and was always welcomed by me and by the students. When the time came for formal observations, this principal had a relationship with the events that occurred within our four walls each day. His appearance at the door for the observation was easily accepted by our classroom.

The feeling of insecurity surrounding the first principal was replaced by a strong feeling of security with the second principal. This confidence in the second principal resulted from a conscious effort on his part. Regular visibility was a priority for him. He made sure that being in and out of classrooms was part of his daily routine. These visits always lifted my spirits and made me see that he cared about instruction.

This also sent a strong message to the children about their learning. They knew he was watching and realized that their principal found importance in their work. Many times, as he did his regular lunch supervision, I would hear him talking to individual students about what he had seen them doing in the classroom—comments relating to instruction, not discipline. Sometimes he would even make cafeteria announcements about class projects he observed. He encouraged the other students to view bulletin boards and displays of this work. His intent was always to keep learning and sharing knowledge as a primary goal of the school. Needless to say…he succeeded.

CLIMATE CAN MAKE A DIFFERENCE

We are all aware that positive staff morale has a high correlation with a positive school climate. If the climate of a building is upbeat, enthusiastic, and productive, then the staff within the building finds it an honest pleasure to come to work. If the climate is negative and full of tension, it eventually will exhaust any positive energies that might have been present. This, of course, leaves nothing left for the students and the wellness of the school.

TEACHER CLIMATE

The establishment of an environment that allows teachers to develop and blossom as leaders is critical to the culturing of faculty to assume increased responsibility. The principal's role in providing this environment, or climate, is essential. Allowing and supporting teachers to assume the reins of leadership is directly affected by the climate established within a school.

According to Keefe, Kelley, and Miller (1985), for a school to be productive, a number of elements must be present. Two of these essential elements of an effective school are a positive school learning climate and a principal who supports the establishment and maintenance of this climate (p. 71).

Although the word "climate" was not used in the literature until the 1950s, "the development of climate as a concept separate from morale is based on the work of H. A. Murray during the 1930s" (Kelley 1980, p. 7). Murray described behavior as "a function of the relationship between the person and his environment" and the relationship between the environment and the person as "that which exists between the 'needs' of the individual and the 'press' (organizational needs and expectations of the environment)" (cited in Kelley 1980, p. 7).

Climate has been defined in several ways. Norton (1984) defined climate as "the collective personality of a school or enterprise, the atmosphere as characterized by the social and professional interactions of the individuals in the school" (p. 43).

According to Sargeant, "climate may be pictured as a personality sketch of a school. As personality describes an individual, so climate defines the essence of an institution" (as cited in Norton, p. 43).

Curran (1983) listed eleven characteristics of an effective school. Included in these was a positive school climate, citing Kelley's 1980 description of school climate and the role of the principal in relation to school climate. Kelley described the relationship as follows:

> It is the principal's function to develop or maintain a positive school climate where teachers can work and students can learn. Because individuals and groups differ in their values and perceptions of what is valuable and meaningful, they also differ in their descriptions of what climate conditions or outcomes are most important. Leadership for climate improvement requires skills in responding to concerns, expectations, and existing conditions or initiating new expectations and

conditions. The ultimate purpose is the improvement of learning. The principal, more than any other individual, is responsible for a school's climate. The teacher has the same responsibility and accountability in the classroom (cited in Curran, p.72).

Though climate has been defined in a variety of ways, there is no dispute that the individual most responsible for the environment developed within an educational setting is the principal. Being sensitive to and working to cultivate the type of environment that promotes risk-taking, change, and teacher input and leadership is of great value to a school.

In the book *Handbook for Conducting School Climate Improvement Projects*, Howard, Howell, and Brainard (1987) identified eight indicators of school climate:

1. **Respect.** All members of the school must be treated with respect and see themselves as persons of worth. An atmosphere of mutual respect prevails.

2. **Caring.** Individuals in the school should feel that people are concerned about them and interested in their wellbeing.

3. **High morale.** School members feel good about what is happening, are willing to perform assigned tasks, and are confident, cheerful, and self-disciplined.

4. **Opportunities for input.** Everyone in the school should be given the opportunity to contribute ideas and know they have been considered.

5. **Continuous academic and social growth.** Both students and faculty strive to develop their skills and knowledge. The professional staff holds high expectations for students.

6. **School renewal.** The school is self-renewing; it is growing, developing, and changing.

7. **Cohesiveness.** School members should feel a sense of belonging to the school. This will result in school spirit or esprit de corps.

8. **Trust.** Individuals within the school must have confidence that others can be counted on to do what they say they will do. Integrity is an essential characteristic of school members (p. 7).

The authors discuss the fact that their extensive experience with climate improvement leads them to believe that "nothing of substance improves until the school's climate does" (p. 50). People's feelings about their school can encourage or impede change. As a school's climate improves there will be fewer discipline problems, better attendance, improved achievement, dropout decline, more respect for and help to others, and a collective responsibility for the wellbeing of the school.

Climate is a reflection of organizational structure and gives a school its own unique personality. School climate can determine the success or failure of a school. A positive climate promotes and breeds a successful outlook and atmosphere. Effective schools create and maintain climates that are comfortable, pleasant, and orderly. They consistently promote high expectations of staff and students (Stronge and Jones 1991).

Winter and Sweeney (1994) discuss the fact that there are many useful ways to measure school climate, but little has been learned about how to develop a climate that is positive. After the authors interviewed 32 teachers about climate, a common strand emerged. The teachers felt that the principal played the most important role in fashioning a school's climate. The teachers felt that the support a principal provided was a key to the climate of the school. The interviews led to the identification of five types of administrative support that affect school climate: recognizing achievement, backing up teachers, encouraging teachers, caring, and administering school rules fairly. This support, caring, and recognition will promote a sense of pride that will lead to a more positive climate. Teachers surrounded by this environment will give the most of their time and talents.

How Can a Leader Affect Climate?

In a study of over 230 elementary school in Indiana, Whitaker (1997) identified four schools with "more positive" climates and four schools with "less positive" climates. Teachers rated the climate in their schools using the Instructional Climate Inventory (Form T) development by MetriTech, Inc. (Maehr and Ames 1988). Each group of four schools included urban, suburban, small-town, and rural schools.

On-site visits and interviews with teachers and the principals were conducted. The following are the themes that emerged as the data was analyzed. These findings are directly related to practices of the principals in the designated buildings. They revealed eight key differences between the principals of the schools with "more positive" climates and the principals of the schools with "less positive" climates:

1. **Responsibility for the climate.** Principals of more positive schools tended to see themselves as responsible for the climate of the building. Principals of the less positive schools often focused on the entire staff as being responsible for the school climate.

2. **Visibility.** Principals and teachers in the more positive schools saw the principal being visible during the day as an important aspect of their building climate. The less positive schools found the principal in his office doing paperwork and in front of the computer a large portion of the day. This was perceived by both the principals and the teachers.

3. **Knowledge of staff beyond school.** The principals of the more positive schools felt that being personally concerned and knowledgeable about the teachers' lives outside of school was an important part of their job in cultivating climate. This attribute was not focused on by any of the principals of the less positive schools.

4. **Regular communication.** The principals of the more positive schools supplied staff with a daily or weekly memo. This memo was motivational as well as informational. The more positive schools' teachers enjoyed and looked forward to this regular correspondence. One of the less positive principals

also used this tool, but it was solely informational and sometimes contained problems and negative situations. The school's teachers were critical of the format and believed that it could be written in a more productive fashion.

5. **Positive and productive staff meetings.** The more positive school principals used staff meetings for purposeful discussions and consensus-building exercises. The less positive schools either did not have faculty meetings or used them basically for sharing logistics and dates.

6. **Knowledge of teacher strengths.** The more positive schools' principals were very aware of teachers' individual strengths and designed individual staff development for them. These principals were aware of different teaching styles and respected teachers for their variety of approaches. The less positive schools' principals did not express awareness of these issues and spoke of teachers grouped more into negative and positive teachers.

7. **Role modeling.** The more positive schools' teachers and principals discussed the important role of the principal in modeling for both faculty and students. One principal discussed how important it was to "walk the talk." The less positive schools' teachers were concerned that the principal's negative attitude filtered down to the teachers and eventually the students. This produced a negative effect on the entire school population.

8. **Attractive physical environment.** Each of the more positive schools was visually neat, attractive, and student-oriented. These schools had purposefully worked on an external "homey" feeling in their physical plant. Three of the four less positive schools appeared dirty, inadequately maintained, and stark of student work. The hallways were bare and in some cases unclean.

When determining the chapters and content of this book, we brainstormed what we felt should be present in the book independent of this study. As we began to look at this research, we realized how the book closely relates to each individual finding from the study. Role modeling is addressed in Chapter 4, staff meetings in Chapter 10, regular written communication in Chapter 6, personal interest in Chapter 14 and the physical environment in Chapter 16. I would like to use the other two areas (visibility and knowledge of teacher strengths) to provide a template for the ideas presented in the rest of this chapter.

Visibility

I don't believe any of you would dispute the statement that your physical, visible presence as the leader has a powerful effect upon the school. I'm sure that many of your teachers have told you that the students just kind of "sense" when you are not around and push their behaviors to different limits. I can remember when I was a teacher thanking a principal for walking down the hall one day. It was a class interchange time when I worked very hard to keep my students orderly and quiet, while some of my colleagues did not. He observed this mixture of order and chaos for a few moments. He then quieted the entire hall and took that time to compliment my class in a very effective and sincere fashion. He then turned and walked away. Never did he reprimand the other classes, but the power of sincere praise to my class made the others (teachers and students) work harder at the appropriate behavior. Being around makes many differences—both large and small.

How do you make yourself more visible? The many needs of the school community pull you in a thousand different directions each day. It is very easy to find yourself scheduled into your office for every minute of your working day. Being "out and about" takes planning and purpose. If you don't *make* it happen, it won't happen. Here are some ideas that might help make visibility a priority in your day.

Good Morning!

Take the time to be at the front doors or outside as the buses drop off students. Greet students with a smile and let them know you are glad they are here. Many times you will also have the opportunity to wave or speak to parents. This visibility is valued and important to parents, too.

In turn, make sure to offer this same greeting to your faculty. Your smiling face and kind words of welcome at the beginning of each day can help them focus on school and the excitement of teaching. You will find that this exercise is healthy for you, too. You are being positive and upbeat. What a perfect way to start your day!

STROLLING THE SCHOOL

In your planner, set aside times each day to be outside your office interacting with the learning community in your school. Many principals do this first thing each morning. Things are usually calmer in the office and getting away is easier. Having children and teachers see you in the morning, smiling and energetic, will set a positive tone for the day. Other principals like to do this after lunch, as an afternoon energizer. After a morning full of meetings and discipline, what a wonderful boost for the afternoon—a way to get a perspective on all that is "right" about the school. There is something magical about observing quality teaching and learning. It will always motivate the true educator!

I have also known principals that schedule "office-free" days—days planned and arranged so that they are not in the office at all. The secretary and staff know this in advance; this helps cut down discipline traffic in the office and allows the secretary to redirect or reschedule phone calls or appointments. Principals who practice this say that the teachers look forward to this day with the knowledge that their leader is living and breathing the day-to-day life of school with them in their territory.

HAVE FUN IN THE CAFETERIA!

I often hear principals lament about cafeteria duty or say with pride that they have hired someone else to manage the cafeteria. Those who lament are wasting a valuable opportunity, and those who have hired someone else should still be in and out of the cafeteria regularly. Why? Lunch is usually a time greatly anticipated by all. The students and teachers are hungry and ready for a break from learning. This is an opportunity for socializing and for replenishing of our bodies' resources. Effective principals take advantage of this time. They might serve the mashed potatoes one day, punch lunch tickets the next. They use this time to talk informally with students and staff. One principal I worked for shared a daily joke with the students in the lunchroom, even letting them rate it via applause. Another chose to praise specific classrooms for projects or assignments she had seen in their rooms during her morning stroll. One principal eats lunch in a designated area of the cafeteria with one class at a time. Conversation is casual, and these students feel quite special during their luncheon date with the principal. This is a wonderful time to learn more about the children and let them hear how much you value their learning and intellectual growth.

BE SEEN WHERE YOU'RE LEAST EXPECTED

When's the last time you played kickball, basketball, chess, or four-square? Get out on that playground, into the commons or the gymnasium! The exercise would do your mind and body good, and participating in play lets your students see the "child" in you. You can informally observe social behaviors of students and talk to them in a more relaxed setting. This also gives you the opportunity to view your playground equipment first-hand to check for safety and proper maintenance.

Many times our only interaction with some students occurs within the four walls of the office for disciplinary purposes. Often observing and communicating with these students in a different setting can provide insight into a child's personality and can help you establish a more productive relationship with them. Being in the hallways between classes, chatting with students in the commons area during lunch, and strolling the campus before and after school make you visible and provide opportunities to observe students in a more comfortable, relaxed setting.

How many of you get immediate headaches as bus discipline reports begin to appear? Riding the school bus periodically can curb the flow of these time-consuming nuisances. Your ride gives you a chance to experience this from the child's point of view and your presence helps them to see that the bus ride is an extension of the school day. You can also model appropriate disciplinary practices for bus drivers. Remember, these folks are not trained educators and need to be able to focus on the driving, not the management. They often don't know how to deal with students and use ineffective techniques to maintain control. You can model and share helpful tips and hints for them while your presence provides them support. In addition, take a moment to imagine the supper table conversations that evening—"Hey, Mom and Dad, guess who rode my bus today?!"

As we discussed in Chapter 1, attention is a very positive reinforcer for everyone. Your active presence in the cafeteria, on the school bus, and on the playground can mean a lot to the adults that regularly serve in these duties. It is also a perfect chance for you to express your thanks for their daily efforts. Not only will the students talk about it at the supper table—so will the bus drivers in the bus barn!

THE "EXTRA" EXTRACURRICULAR ACTIVITIES

Of course, we all know that attending our school's extracurricular activities is an important and necessary feature of being the school principal. There are also opportunities to share social time with your students at outside activities not related to school. Many students are involved in sports-related activities beyond the school realm. Get schedules and event dates from students and parents. Try to attend a few of these "extra" functions each year. These are times you can actually relax and enjoy watching students because you are not in charge. It might even be an event that your whole family would enjoy—a dance recital, soccer game, area festival, or community picnic.

You also have the opportunity to give praise and recognition to the sponsors of these activities. The more you are there, the more specific opportunities for reinforcement you will have. You do not have to be the building principal to practice these types of activities. Attending coworkers' clubs and events can be very reinforcing. No matter what your role is in the school, people value and appreciate your taking the time to support and be there for them. Any educational leader can help boost the morale of others by showing support for their activities.

FIND YOUR PLACE IN CLASSROOMS

In all honesty, being in classrooms was by far the most exciting and invigorating part of my day. Immersing yourself in classrooms allows you to feel the heart of the school beating. You can see the science experiment in fourth grade, join a literature discussion group in third grade, participate in the mind-bender in second grade, listen to children's writing in first grade, play the triangle in music, or just sit back and watch a master teacher at work. This is not formal evaluation time. Your visit should not be punitive or obtrusive in nature. This is time for you to connect with the inner spirit of your school. Being in classrooms regularly can give you a broader understanding of your school's purpose, personality, and performance.

These classroom visits vary in length of time and in what you do during your stay. Sometimes you will be the quiet observer, watching and soaking up the teaching and learning. Other times you will find yourself a participant in the lesson or activity. Some visits may last only a few minutes, others longer. Let the nature of the lesson or activity guide how long you choose to linger.

As you walk in, let yourself relax into the climate of the room. Don't be in your evaluation mode. You are an educator and a lifelong learner. Model this for your students and staff. On some days you may jot down notes about specific positive educational practices you observe. Share these with the appropriate teachers through a note of praise or informal conversation about what you saw that exemplified quality teaching and learning. These simple gestures mean so much to teachers.

NOW HEAR THIS! THE MORNING ANNOUNCEMENTS

Many schools choose to begin their day with the morning announcements, and many principals give these announcements. This is fine, but I would encourage the principals to involve children and staff members, too. Have children read the menu, daily weather, thoughts for the day, school pledge, or begin the pledge of allegiance for the entire school. Student participation can begin as early as first grade and extend through high school. It can even involve two to three students each morning who divide these duties. A standard form (Figure 4) can be used each day, and the students arrive at the office in the morning with their parts filled out. The teacher can assist younger students in filling out the form and being prepared to present their portion. Middle school and high school students can assume this responsibility themselves. This gives students the opportunity to practice public speaking though a unique medium and can be very motivational. You will find that many parents even stop by on their way to work to hear their child do the morning announcements! Principals can still be a part of the morning procedure, providing the part(s) they feel would be the most effective. Invite teachers to share announcements pertinent to them whenever appropriate. The school community hears from both students and the school leader each morning. What a powerful message this can send each and every day—this school is child-centered and has a leader who cares.

THE ULTIMATE BIRTHDAY TREAT!

Many principals offer a 30-minute respite to teachers as a birthday treat. This is a kind and appreciated gesture, but also the opportunity for the principal to interact with students and faculty in their daily school routine. The students can see you as an instructor, and the teachers are reminded that you haven't forgotten how to manage and educate children. Again, this provides an opportunity to experience the heart and soul of your school while making a teacher feel appreciated.

I knew of a dynamic superintendent who, as part of the fundraising drive for a local charity, would put the names of all staff members who donated into a jar for a drawing. He would then select several staff members' names and take over their duties for an hour as a reward to the lucky ones who were chosen. There were always pictures in the paper of him serving mashed potatoes in a cafeteria, or reading to kindergarten students, as he fulfilled his obligations. What a positive tone this set for the district!

Along this same line, I know of a principal who periodically substitutes as the crossing guard at various school intersections. This provides visibility to the community, parents, students, and teachers while the modeling emphasizes the importance of safety

FIGURE 4

Morning Announcements

(template for daily use)

Announcer # 1   (Name: _____)

Good Morning!

* Today is _____(i.e. - Thursday)_____ , _____(i.e. - September 25)_____ , _(i.e. - current year)_ , and the official time is _____(i.e. - 8:07 a.m.)_____ .

* The announcements are brought to you today by ___(i.e. - Mrs.Foster's)___ class. _____(i.e. - David Small)_____ , _____(i.e. - Suzie Fry)_____ , and_____ (i.e. - Mike Smith)_____ reporting.

* The weather for today is _____(i.e. - cloudy, high of 78 degrees)_____ .

Announcer #2 (Name: _____)

* The menu for today is:

* The Word of the Week is:

* The Author of the Month Clue is:

Announcer #3 (Name: _____)

* Announcements:

* Our Thought for the Day Is: _____
_____
_____

Please Stand for the Pledge of Allegiance and the School Pledge.

at each school crossing. It can also be a morale boost to our important crossing guards!

KNOWLEDGE OF TEACHERS' STRENGTHS

Understanding and appreciating the talents that staff members bring to your school setting is an important part of the educational leader's job. Each individual is unique and has distinctive talents. Cultivating these talents is not the sole job of the teacher alone. You must provide inspiration, support, and opportunities to teachers as they work toward refining and sharing their strengths. Perhaps some of the following ideas will motivate you to support each individual teacher in the quest for knowledge and professional growth.

PASS IT ON

One way to help individual staff members to grow and know that you are aware of their strengths is to share your mountains of mail and literature with them. As you sort through your incoming mail, keep your teachers in mind. When a flyer about an exciting multiple-intelligences workshop crosses your desk, share it with the teacher(s) interested in this area. Staff members will be pleased that you are thinking about them and are aware of their professional growth interests.

As you read professional journals, keep mental notes of outstanding articles to share with staff members. Copy these and put them in the teacher's box with a short note explaining that you thought of them when reading this article. Many teachers appreciate this "filtering" of the masses of publications. They don't have time to read as much as they should, but when the principal shares current articles, they can spend time on something that has already impacted an educator they respect. They know the information will broaden their knowledge and won't be a waste of their reading time. If an article applies to a school-wide goal or is of great interest to all staff, attach a copy to your weekly memo so everyone can read and learn.

In our increasingly techno-savvy world, many schools have e-mail capabilities. E-mailing teaching strategies, management tips, quotes, and suggested book or article titles to staff (individuals or the whole group) is also an effective tool to engage teachers in their individual and collective professional growth.

INSPIRATION STATION

Many principals suggest particular books to staff and some will even purchase books for resource purposes. A professional resource library can become an integral part of staff growth in a school setting. This collection of books, journals, videos, and brochures will be well used by a staff whose principal thoughtfully purchases resources and designs the environment that houses them. One principal calls this the Inspiration Station. She has lined a wall in a small conference room with shelves that store the materials. Everything is well labeled and easy to locate. Attractive and inspirational posters cover the wall space. A bulletin board placed above the shelves is her spot to post brochures for upcoming workshops and professional growth experiences. She has even designed a comfortable place for teachers to read in this room. Two cushioned chairs flanking a table with a reading lamp on it create an inviting area to peruse the resources from the Inspiration Station. If space is an issue, some principals have designated a part of the library for this purpose, or even some shelves in a storage closet! Just make the area accessible and attractive, and update resources regularly. When you purchase new resources, bring them to a faculty meeting and show them to everyone while providing a brief overview of what the book or video has to offer.

LET THEM KNOW YOU NOTICE

Acknowledging what you see and approve of can greatly influence teachers' work. In a study conducted with more than 1,800 teachers (Blase and Kirby 1992), it was found that teachers perceived personal compliments and individual attention from their principals as key elements to their motivation and success in the classroom. These forms of acknowledgement take time, but it is time well spent.

Keep a note pad with you at all times. When you see something inspirational in a classroom, write a note of praise for the teacher while you are in the room itself. Place it on the teacher's desk as you leave, or put it in their mailbox when you return to the office. Some principals jot notes of praise on Post-It Notes and place them on the teacher's desk or plan book before they exit the classroom. In the quiet hours before the school's open house, one principal traveled to every classroom, leaving a short Post-It Note of thanks and inspiration on each teacher's desk. The note greeted each teacher that evening and provided motivation to "shine" for the night's events. Many teachers keep the notes of encouragement forever and read them periodically for a spirit boost. Most importantly, you are acknowledging what they do well and this inspires them to continue their quest for effective teaching strategies.

As we discussed in Chapter 6, another creative way to praise teachers is through your weekly memo. Give credit to staff members who are going above and beyond. Mentioning their names in the weekly memo provides them a pat on the back and allows others in the building the knowledge of the success of a peer. Celebrating successes as a team can be an important part of shared growth as a school.

Whenever you have a superior (superintendent, assistant superintendent, director) in the building, use their presence to your advantage. Share the accomplishments of your faculty with the superintendent while the staff members are present. Make this exchange of information brief, but sincere. The superior will appreciate the knowledge and the staff member will feel great.

LET THE EXPERT BE A GUIDE

When there is expertise in your building, use it! This wonderful wealth of knowledge can be used to move your school or team forward and can provide an important niche of belonging and contribution for the staff member deemed an expert. Please don't feel that because I am using this word, you have to call them experts to their faces. Many teachers will feel uncomfortable with this term. Just give them the regard and acknowledgement they deserve because of their area of strength. Let these people guide and inform inservice committees. As your school begins to design staff or team professional development, use these people to share their wisdom, to suggest speakers and resources, and even to be presenters. These "experts" can also give mini-presentations at faculty or department meetings and share with their peers through your weekly memo. A short paragraph submitted by them describing a teaching strategy or new assessment approach can yield great benefits.

It is also important to encourage these people to share their teaching successes with others outside your school. Encourage them to present at regional, state, and national conferences. Share the guidelines for submitting presentation topics and offer your assistance in writing the proposal. Perhaps you even have money available to assist in their travel expenses if they are accepted to present. Presenting at conferences can reaffirm their commitment and boost morale significantly. Encourage everyone in the building to celebrate their success if they are accepted. They will be representing the entire school and it is a wonderful opportunity for other educators to view your building in a positive and upbeat way.

Some of these teachers will also be interested in writing grants. Many grants provide funds for teaching resources, money to attend conferences, and funds to pay stipends for summer work. Identify the individuals you feel have the time, talents, and energy to write a grant proposal, and talk to them individually. Get a sense of their interest level. For some, the task may seem overwhelming. Make sure they know this is fine and that you don't want to overburden them. Others will see the challenge as exciting and motivating. Send these people to grant-writing workshops, let them read former accepted grants, and allow them to confer with other grant writers in the building or school district. The actual writing of the grant can sometimes allow these people to really internalize what they have accomplished and where they are headed. If the grant is awarded, it's time for celebration! Acknowledge the success of hard work and enjoy using the extra funds to further the learning opportunities for the students in your building.

Most of all, don't be afraid to let these people help *you* learn. Just being the leader of the organization doesn't make you an expert on everything. Admit you are a lifelong learner and open your mind to the great things these staff members can teach you. Ask them questions, go to them for curricular suggestions, and thank them for what they give your department or building. Let them know that their contributions are appreciated and that you continue to learn so much from them.

GROWTH OF THE INDIVIDUAL

It is important to know that as we understand, appreciate, and utilize teacher strengths, we must also nurture their growth as individual professionals. One of the first steps in helping a person grow is providing opportunity for the individual to reflect or self-evaluate. This can take many forms. Some principals have staff members complete learning-styles questionnaires for themselves. This helps teachers identify their styles and begin to think about how their style might influence their teaching and students' learning.

One very popular way of reflection lies in the development of a professional portfolio. As described by Campbell, Cignetti, Melenyzer, Nettles, and Wyman (1997),

> A portfolio is an organized, goal-driven documentation of your professional growth and achieved competence in the complex act called teaching. Although it is a collection of documents, a portfolio is tangible evidence of the wide range of knowledge, dispositions, and skills that you possess as a growing professional. What's more, documents in the portfolio are self-selected, reflecting your individuality and autonomy" (p. 3).

Many school leaders encourage staff members to create portfolios. This gives the staff member the opportunity to pull together evidence of teaching excellence and reflect upon success and growth. It is important to note that school leaders that encourage this type of portfolio are also building their own. This models for staff that they are willing to compile artifacts and analyze their own professional growth and competence.

Yearly goal action plans or Professional Development Plans (PDPs) are excellent avenues for teachers to grow in their knowledge and pedagogy. PDPs, further described in Chapter 9, are simple individual growth plans designed by staff members with support and assistance from the school leader. The plan sets forth the desired professional goal, a plan for achieving it, and the opportunity to reflect upon progress during the school year. This gives each staff member the chance to work on an individual area of interest and allows the school leader to be a part of this exciting growth journey.

Peer coaching is another avenue for individual support and development. Teachers helping teachers is one of the most powerful tools in achieving school effectiveness, but often one of the most neglected. The way most schools are structured and organized doesn't allow teachers the time necessary to observe each other and provide feedback. Organizing peer coaching teams within a school can assure that this opportunity for observation will be present and is supported by the school leader.

Interest groups designed to pull together those working on similar goals can stimulate thought and progress among teachers as they work toward a common outcome. These groups allow them to share resources, strategies, and stories of growth and success. The opportunity to share with your peers is a treasured commodity among most educators. You, as the school leader, can design these opportunities. Perhaps you know of four or five teachers working on professional portfolios. Connect them to each other one morning over coffee and doughnuts at your invitation. Encourage them to meet again in a couple of weeks, bringing their "product in progress" so that they can share with each other. Urge the six faculty members working on multiple-intelligences implementation to get together and share ideas. Invite the three teachers studying alternative classroom management plans to report their findings to each other and brainstorm management approaches for future use. These small groups can bring together teachers who might not have normally worked together and encourages the sharing and celebrating of true professional growth.

This chapter has provided many concrete ways you can make a difference each day in the morale of your school. Use the ideas as they are described here, or let them become catalysts for your own creative approach that meets the needs of your staff. Just remember that *what you do* is more important than *how you say it*. The sincere regard you show members of your learning community will provide a powerful model for all those viewing you. I close with a poem you might want to share with your staff, but

as you read this, think of yourself and of the daily impact you
have by the leadership actions that you take.

Dear Teacher

I would rather see a lesson
than to hear one any day;

I'd rather you would walk with me
than merely point the way.

The eye's a better trainer
and more willing than the ear,

and words can be confusing,
but examples always clear.

I can see you when in motion,
but your tongue too fast may run,

I soon can learn to do it
if you'll let me see it done.

The best of all life's teachers
are the ones who live the creed,

To see good put to action
is the model that I need.

The counsel you are giving
may be very fine and true,

But I'd rather get my lesson
by observing what you do.

Author unknown

PART 3

SUPERVISION, EVALUATION, AND . . . MORALE IMPROVEMENT?

8

LEADERSHIP BY WALKING AROUND

The power of presence can never be overstated. This is more than being available and accessible; it is being proactive with all aspects of quality leadership. Being available and being accessible are very important qualities of effective leadership. But these styles by themselves are reactive and put the burden on the staff to approach you. Being visible in classrooms, in the lunchroom, at recess, and in the halls not only takes your accessibility to another level, but puts you in control of interacting with everyone, not just with staff members that come to you. Being "out and about" also provides for opportunities to support, reward, and acknowledge students and teachers in their environment.

"Leadership by walking around" is one of the most important strategies any administrator can use. It shows your interest and support, provides you with first-hand knowledge of what is going on in your building, and increases the number of times you can reinforce specific teaching strategies. It also allows you to model expectations through actions, not words.

Even with all this in mind, we as leaders continue to put being in classrooms on the "back burner" because of unplanned parent meetings, district meetings, discipline situations, and so on. In the early years of my career I was having trouble getting into classrooms. I was a middle school assistant principal and discipline was eating up my entire day. I was visiting with my principal about this problem and his response is something I will always remember. He asked when the last time was that I missed a meeting with the superintendent. As with most of us, my response was that I had not missed a meeting with the superintendent. He then went on to say, "Isn't it as important to be in classrooms as it is to meet with the superintendent?" This reminded me that if I make it a priority, then it will get done. What can be a bigger priority for educational leaders than to be where the action is? This can only increase the effectiveness of the leader, and, above all, increase the quality of education for the students.

The following outline provides ways to manage your time to allow you to be in classrooms, ideas for reinforcement and support while you are in classrooms, and suggestions on how to give teachers additional opportunities and support for improvement.

Finding the Time

Here are some ideas for managing your time so that you can visit classrooms regularly.

Understand that being in classrooms is as important as anything you do, so set time in your planner for visits to classrooms. Getting into classrooms only when you have free time will never work. It is like saving money with anything you have left in the checkbook at the end of the month—it simply will not happen. Just as you tuck your savings away at the beginning of the month, write in your calendar at the start of the week a block of time each day that you will be in classrooms, the lunchroom, the library, or the playground. You might want to write in your calendar, "Tuesday 10–10:30, visit library." Thursday 1–1:30," be on playground." These are not formal evaluations. They can be ten-minute visits or two-minute visits.

Vary your classroom visiting time so you have the opportunity to see different activities and teachers. If you always visit Mrs. Jones at 10:00, you will always see her reading lesson or her third-period class.

If you are in a large building and cannot see every class-room every day, set up a rotation. Otherwise, you will see the same teachers several times and others only a few times. You can plan to see your staff by grade levels, teams, departments, or hallways—whichever works best for you. If your building has three hallways, divide it by hallway. You can also plan to visit two grade levels each day.

Use a simple way to keep track of your visits. Having a checklist of classrooms on your desk is a great idea. Simply check the list to record each room that you have visited. This is also a way you can track your visits. By midyear, you will be surprised at the total, and you will clearly see if you are visiting certain teachers more often than others.

Be in areas when large groups of students are together. This includes the lunchroom, the hallways between classes, recess time for elementary schools, activity areas, the library, or the commons. Many of the "fires" administrators deal with flare up in these areas. Your presence can put them out before they start. Being in the lunchroom might save more time than it takes! An example is dealing with an argument between two students. If you are in the lunchroom, you can handle it with a quick inter-vention by pulling the students out in the hall and reminding them of the consequences of fighting. This may take care of it. On the other hand, if you are not in the lunchroom the argu-ment may escalate into a fight. You might spend the major part of the afternoon finding out the facts, calling parents, and re-solving the issue. The saying "You can pay me now, or pay me later" comes to life here.

Being visible in these areas also allows you to model expec-tations for staff. The example of the boys arguing can illustrate this. First of all, being in the lunchroom shows your commit-ment to kids and that you are willing to assist in any way. The staff can observe how you interact with students and staff. Lunchroom supervisors have the chance to watch an effective and appropriate intervention. This modeling extends far beyond the lunchroom. Word spreads through the building that the leader is out and about and working with kids. This allows you to "walk the walk" of your expectations.

USING THE TIME

Now that you have a plan that allows you the time to "lead by walking around," what are some ideas to use this time effectively and efficiently?

Know that classroom visits may be ten-minute visits or two-minute visits. Set this up by indicating to your teachers that you will try to get into their rooms as often as you can. Let them know that they do not have to do anything special when you visit, such as asking if you need anything. Inform them that if you do need something, you will let them know.

Another way to increase the comfort level of classroom teachers is to inform them that they will know if you are doing a formal evaluation. No matter how often you get into classrooms, teachers like to know when they are being evaluated. This is not to say that you do not have unscheduled evaluations, but if you drop in to evaluate unexpectedly, let them know that you are doing so. When they see you in the classrooms on a regular basis, your visits becomes routine and are not disruptive to the students or the teacher. Because of this, the teachers or students do not feel they need to do anything different if you are in the classroom.

Use this time for specific positive feedback. You can never give too much encouragement. Being out and about provides you with a perfect avenue to give specific feedback. If you are in the lunchroom and see a student who had behavior problems the day before doing a great job today, you can compliment him as he is getting his lunch. In a classroom, offer specific positive comments: "It is amazing how your students handle the transition time between activities." "The way your sophomores developed that rubric really shows how much work you have done with collaborative learning." "The way Tim spoke up in your class meeting was great; I have never heard him speak at all. This really shows how you have established a comfortable and productive climate in your classroom." Such statements are much more meaningful than something like "nice job," or "you're good with kids." Central office personnel, department chairs, all of us in education benefit from receiving and/or giving specific praise.

Carry a pad of "sticky" notes with you at all times. If you do not enjoy using this type of paper, use a small notepad or the like. Develop the habit of writing notes to yourself to compliment a teacher or a student later. For instance, I might jot down "Mrs. Richards—Greece/small groups/maps/Jim Smith." My note shows up later that day in her mailbox: "Mrs. Richards, how did you get those third-period seventh graders to work so well in small groups? Jim Smith's group had a great map with unbelievable detail about the rivers of Greece! Thanks for all your good work! Have a nice day." This note accomplishes several positive things. It shows my interest in specific points in the class. It also shows Mrs. Richards that I appreciate and value her. In addition, this type of note makes the writer feel as good as the receiver.

Write a note to a teacher or student and put it on their door or desk. This strategy is very efficient, productive, and quick. This also is an easy avenue to communicate with students. For example, "Mary, I enjoyed watching your students do their president presentations. Your students were so relaxed speaking in front of the class. Katherine and Mariah's use of PowerPoint was impressive. Our school is better because of you. Have a great day!" This note, which took approximately sixty seconds to write, had many positive outcomes. First, it reinforced high expectations by mentioning the kids being relaxed and the use of PowerPoint. Second, it was specific, using students' names and a particular activity to add "meat" to the note. Third, it ended with a statement of support and acknowledgement for the teacher. As mentioned previously, a note like this is also a "pick-me-up" for the writer. I have had teachers tell me, "This is the first positive note I have received in twenty-five years of teaching," and "The note you gave me not only made my day, but made my week." When we talk about efficient use of time, getting this many positive results from a sixty-second investment is something that cannot be ignored. It is also fun to do!

Fill out forms, set up meeting agendas, outline grants, and so forth in the classrooms. As we all know, our time is very valuable. If we are not careful, paperwork and putting out fires can take all of our time. This also means that we can literally be in our office everyday the rest of our careers. I have yet to meet people in education that have indicated that they have too much time with nothing to do. Because of this, we have to be conscious of our priorities and try to do everything we can to be in the classrooms. Taking work into the classroom is easier now than ever before. With tools such as laptop computers, you can be mobile, not tied to your office. Anything you need to do on a computer can now be done in the classroom. Examples of work you can accomplish during classroom visits include writing notes to teachers that you have visited, composing form letters to be sent home to parents, writing your weekly memo, filling out educational surveys, developing staff agendas, reviewing notes taken at a district administrators' meeting, writing your personal professional growth plan, and reading educational material. This list can go on and on.

The point is, except for accessing e-mail and attending private meetings, you do not need to be in your office. Admittedly, it might be more convenient to be there, but this is not the most effective way to lead an organization. Doing work in the rooms has many positive outcomes. First, of course, you are more visible. Also, when you are away from your phone, and therefore not "on call" to put out small fires that can be addressed at a later time, you have more opportunities to reinforce and interact with staff and students. Managing your time like this allows you to get a lot of work done away from your desk. Furthermore, being out and about can be a great "shot in the arm" during a stressful day. Above all, getting out of the office allows you to be around young people on a regular basis.

Sort your mail in the lunchroom. The goal of this strategy is to "kill two birds with one stone." As principal or assistant principal, you know that issues are more likely to arise during certain activities and times of the day—and lunchroom time is one of these. If you are there, you can eliminate some of the problems before they start. Furthermore, eating lunch together is an important part of our day and offers great opportunities for interacting with students and teachers. But the fact that you are in the lunchroom does not mean you cannot get anything else done. Pull up a trash can and sort through your mail, throwing out all the "junk" and prioritizing your legitimate mail. This simple idea can save you 10 to 15 minutes every day. That might not seem like much, but in a nine-month school year, you can save 45 hours!

Use the library for your quiet work. For work that you need uninterrupted time to complete, find a spot in the library. This not only gives you a quiet place to work, but also puts you where you are visible to potentially every student and teacher. In addition, you can model behavioral expectations of what the library is for.

Eat in the lunchroom or on the playground. This is a great time to visit with students. In addition, you can model the importance of a comfortable climate by laughing with students and being with teachers in a relaxed everyday situation. This is also a time for everyone to see how you interact with the paraprofessionals, custodial staff, and cafeteria staff. Your actions show that you are accessible and that you respect everyone in the school. In addition, you are able to see the students, and the students are able to see you, in an unstructured situation. This can be very informative about how students interact and communicate with each other, and may give you many opportunities to interact with them.

Use this time to take breaks from your desk. As we have noted, being in your office can eat up your entire day, every day. Given the mountain of day-to-day activities in education, you do not have, or want to take, many unproductive breaks. Any time you leave your desk, you most likely are thinking that you should be getting back to work. To combat this feeling, take your 'breaks" to play a game at recess, read to students in the classroom, or eat with the students. This gets you out of your office to do something other than routine work; it puts you in situations where you can interact with students and staff; and above all, it gives you opportunities to just have fun at work. All of these benefits can rejuvenate you so the rest of the day can be more productive and enjoyable.

THE GIFT OF TIME

When you have developed the habit of being out and about, you can give teachers extra opportunities by introducing some of the following activities.

On parent-teacher conference nights, take students for the last period of the day, giving teachers a short break during this 12-hour work day. This may seem like a monumental task. But the truth is, it can be done, and it is terrific for staff morale.

The first step is to look for possible ways to make this happen. For example, in a K–5 elementary, you can start by having the fifth grade students be the leaders of this activity. This can be a great student morale builder. Divide each fifth grade class into four leadership teams. You can do this at random or according to the grade level each student is interested in working with. The classroom teacher can also help to determine which students will work with which grade levels. In a three-section building (that is, three classes at each grade level) you will have twelve groups of four to seven fifth grade students. Each of these groups will be in charge of a class. This will give you a fifth grade group to cover each of the twelve classes in grades one through four. To address the kindergarten classes, you can use four to six fifth grade students to help with each class. This will make all of the leadership teams smaller, which in turn gives them more responsibility, which is very effective in showing the fifth grade students how important they are in the success of the school.

Once the leadership teams have been assigned to specific classes, your next step is to meet with them in advance to discuss possible activities they might do with the younger students. This can be done when they are all together at lunch or during another time that does not take away from academics.

At that meeting, you can assign specific areas of the playground for each grade level and develop possible activities. You should also talk about what is expected when you escort the students to and from their regular classrooms. After assigning the student teams, you can make a quick-and-easy chart showing which students are working with which classes and where each group will be on the playground.

This procedure might also involve all non-homeroom staff members—paraprofessional, physical education, music, art, and special education staff. It may seem that getting support staff to buy in to this idea at your school would be very challenging. However, this may not always be the case. A successful approach might be to work by yourself the first time you try this, covering all of the classes with only the fifth grade students to assist you. When the support staff see that it actually can be done and that you are willing to take all 400 students by yourself, they are very likely to join you within a few minutes, asking how they can help. These efforts on their part, even if only a few of them initiate these supporting roles, provide another opportunity to reinforce their efforts at being team players.

Before the next parent-teacher conference, you can have a quick meeting with any support staff to outline the supervision plan and to discuss the best way to supervise this 45-minute period. This group of adults can choose what grade they would most like to work with and provide input on appropriate activities. There are many benefits to letting them choose and provide input. They may know a certain grade level better than another, or they may want to work with another adult that they are comfortable with, and so on. The point is that they have freedom to choose. You will be amazed at the positive response you and the non-homeroom staff will get from the homeroom teachers.

You may think this is a lot of planning just to give teachers a 45-minute break. In our experience, however, the positive outcomes of such an activity start with the break, but they do not end with it. The actual planning of the first "teacher break" is somewhat time-consuming, but once the plan is in place you can simply make some fine-tuning adjustments to the original plan. As the idea becomes more familiar, teachers will automatically divide their kids up, the support staff will decide which activity they want to supervise, and the rest of the building will know what to expect. Eventually, it will almost run itself. Middle and high schools can put this plan into action using student council leaders, grade-level teams, or subject-area teams. It can work effectively at any level.

Organizing this type of teacher support activity yields many benefits. It shows the teachers that their time and efforts are appreciated. It promotes cross-grade activities that enhance the positive leadership roles of the older students and increase the "team" spirit among students. It also provides all non-homeroom staff with an easy, non-threatening way to support the classroom teacher. In addition, it increases appreciation from the classroom teachers for the work and care of the support staff. It also keeps you as the leader out of the "I am doing this great thing" posture, and shows the "we are in this together" attitude. Most importantly, teachers will never forget this type of support, which can enhance staff togetherness and the morale of the staff for the rest of the school year and beyond.

During teacher appreciation week, give teachers "the gift of time" by teaching their classes. Through the years, educational leaders have tried many things—everything from nice notes, to small gifts, to food—to show teachers how much their efforts are appreciated. All of these are appropriate and do show appreciation. An additional idea you might want to try is "the gift of time."

There are many ways to do this. During the month that includes teacher appreciation week, give every teacher a certificate acknowledging their efforts and accomplishments. In addition, provide a note of thanks explaining that they have been given "the gift of time." You can use the same certificate for every teacher. This saves time and still gets the point across. Here's a sample of such a certificate:

The Gift of Time

In appreciation of your efforts and accomplishments, I will take your class for one hour, during which you may do whatever you please. Please schedule this time with your grade-level (or department or interdisciplinary) team so that I can take all of the students in that team at the same time, so we do not disrupt anyone else's schedule.

To give you the maximum break, I encourage you to take this time at the beginning of the day, around lunch, or at the end of the day. This time is for you, so you can go out for lunch with your team, sleep in, or leave early; it is not so you can get additional work done. So, no grading papers, reviewing files, or planning lessons allowed!

This type of appreciation is very powerful. I have found that many teachers will arrange to go out to lunch together. This is a nice break, and it gives time for staff to be together and talk. I do not know of a better way to show appreciation and increase staff morale than to give "the gift of time."

Have new teachers evaluate *you* teaching a lesson so they become familiar with the evaluation process and so you can demonstrate your willingness to work and learn together. When new staff start in a building they, like all of us, have some trepidation about being evaluated and what it will mean to them. As leaders who understand this, one of our goals is to make those teachers feel as comfortable as possible. A way to address this is to visit with them to explain the evaluation process. To carry this a step further, have new staff evaluate you teaching a lesson.

To set this up, meet with the new teachers and discuss what the observation and evaluation process is all about. Help them understand that this process is a tool for growth for both the person being evaluated and the evaluator. This is paramount to the effectiveness of the process. Most new teachers would like to hear this philosophy, but will still be apprehensive about being evaluated.

To advance to the next level of comfort and understanding, it can be very beneficial to have the new teacher evaluate you while you teach a lesson. First, have a pre-evaluation meeting with the teacher to discuss the lesson. You can offer to teach a lesson developed by the teacher or you can create one yourself, depending on what the teacher wants to do.

The next step is to teach the lesson. The strength of this process comes from your openness. You as principal do not have to teach the perfect lesson. As a matter of fact, discussing the parts of the lesson that did not go so well shows your openness, honesty, and willingness to grow. This models for the teacher that anyone and everyone involved in this process can learn and improve. This also shows that conferencing in a constructive way is not a personal thing but a professional process of improvement. The post-evaluation can be very comfortable if you as the leader openly talk about the lesson.

One example of how to start the post-evaluation conversation could be, "I think the lesson went well, but it took too long to transition from the full-class instruction into the individual projects. How do you think I could have improved?"

This opens the door for the new staff member(s) to give their ideas and suggestions. One thing to keep in mind is that any questions that you present are not intended to find out how much the teacher knows, but to open communication and to increase comfort. With that in mind, keep the questions open and easy to address. This also models that it is OK to be self-critical, and it is also OK to "toot your own horn." The meeting should always end on a positive note. "Thanks for taking the time to let me teach your class," "Your ideas for me to improve are very helpful; they will help me do my job better," and "Our entire building is better because you are on our staff," are examples.

Taking extra time to work with staff new to the building is essential for you as the leader to offer support. The more the new teachers can interact with you, the more they can see what your expectations are and how you interact with teachers; hopefully, this will increase the teacher's comfort level.

Teach classes so that teachers can have the opportunity to observe each other. The more professionals can observe, dialogue, and work with each other, the better the climate, the teamwork, and above all, the students' learning will be. Too many times we say this is true but do not go any farther with it. The obstacles are familiar—not having funds to pay substitutes, not being able to adjust schedules, not allotting enough time. But sometimes leadership means eliminating the reasons *not* to do something, not just focusing on why we *should* do something. If having teachers observe other teachers is a priority, you can make it happen.

As educational leaders, we have the responsibility to continue to improve ourselves and to provide avenues for teachers to improve. A natural way to accomplish both of these is to teach classes ourselves, freeing those teachers to observe others. But how can this be done?

One way is to make this a priority by including the process as a part of your own personal professional development plan. A measurable goal for you is as simple as "All teachers will make at least one observation of another teacher by the end of the year." Notice that you are not saying they are coaching, reporting back to you, or even discussing what they've observed. Leave this up to the teacher to decide. This will take away some of the apprehension of observing or being observed. Start with teachers visiting whom they want; as teachers become comfortable with this process, move on to additional observations. These opportunities may be used for formal coaching or time to observe a friend teach. The more teachers see each other work, the better students are served in the classroom. After the teachers understand the expectation of visiting another professional, let them set up who, when, and where.

I try to give teachers the first couple of months to set this up and get back to me. Then I work with them to set the date. Please let the teachers know they do not have to make special plans for you. The idea is to make this as easy as possible for the teachers. As you teach in different classrooms, other positive aspects emerge; it shows teachers that you are a hands-on leader who understands what is going on in the "trenches," and even that you are willing to learn something about how you can improve as a teacher. After this activity becomes more comfortable for the teachers in your school, the next step may be to have dialogue groups to discuss these observations.

An additional way to "lead by walking around" is to work with all classified staff. Taking students that a paraprofessional works with, covering the office for your secretary, or helping the custodian are a few examples of working with classified staff. This not only lets the classified staff know how important they are, but it allows the entire staff to observe you working with everyone. This can build the "we're all in this together" attitude that can boost staff morale.

Modeling your expectations for students and staff is another way to capitalize on being out and about. If a discipline situation arises while you are in the lunchroom, deal with it yourself in a positive and efficient way. This one example shows every student in the lunchroom your expectation, and every staff member sees how a negative situation can be handled in a calm positive manner. A proactive approach may be to compliment students for having a good game or helping a younger student with their lunch. This shows students and teachers your positive expectations.

Leading by walking around is a strategy to help improve your effectiveness as an educational leader. It also provides leaders with rewarding and positive experiences every day. The answer to the question "Why be out and about?" is so obvious that now the question is, "Why not?"

9

THE EVALUATION PROCESS—TURNING PAINFUL INTO POSITIVE

The formal evaluation process is an opportunity to raise the morale and self-worth of educational professionals in all of our schools. Too often, however, this process is seen as having little or no value; it can even be a demotivating experience. This is true even with the most talented staff members in our schools. Is there any hope for changing the focus and the end results of evaluation into a more productive and reinforcing one? Well, the focus of this chapter is to reinforce staff morale throughout the evaluation process.

WALKING ON WATER

Many teacher evaluation forms—particularly the end-of-the-year-checklist summative forms—have a list of criteria and then three or more possible rankings for each. An example might be

Teacher is prepared for the lesson. (Check one)

Does not meet expectations ___

Meets expectations ___

Exceeds expectations ___

It is interesting to think through the purpose of the three columns. Which kind of teacher—superstar, backbone, or mediocre—is the "exceeds expectations" column intended to describe? Obviously, the superstar. But think about the feelings of the superstar in relation to this column. If you have 15 criteria on your end-of-the-year checklist, and you give your best teacher "exceeds expectations" for 14 of the items, you probably think that the superstar will feel great after seeing the evaluation instrument. However, which of those 15 criteria will the superstar focus on? The answer, of course, is the one for which they received "meets expectations." Thus, this positive experience becomes a deflator for the very person you were most hoping to reinforce.

This is one reason that our summative end-of-the-year evaluations should not have any responses other than "meets expectations" and "does not meet expectations." You can always add verbal comments in any form you choose as a way to reinforce your best staff members.

TELL ME A LITTLE BIT ABOUT . . .

One of the challenges for a leader is to find the balance between the improvement of faculty members and the support of their morale. In other words, there is potentially a fine line between giving someone a suggestion for improvement and damaging the person's psyche. One way to find the balance is to help people dialogue through the process using self-reflection.

I once had a dynamite assistant principal who always used to say, "You don't have to know anything to ask questions." This approach serves us very well as educational leaders. Let's look at an example involving observing a teacher with less than sterling classroom management skills. If you are in the room and students are in and out of their seats in a disruptive fashion, talking to each other in a distracting manner, or even laying their heads on the desks sleeping, you have some choices to make in terms of communicating your concerns to this teacher.

You may be tempted to initiate a post-observation conversation by using judgments. Statements like "The students in your room seemed out of control" or "You need to have better classroom management" may be true, but they set up a conversation for confrontation, defensiveness, or both. Instead of initiating the conversation in this judgmental fashion, you might try asking a question. "Tell me a little bit about Jimmy and Bryan getting out of their desks during class," or "Does Johnny usually lay his head on the desk during class?" can provide an opportunity for them to do the majority of the dialoguing. You can then steer the conversation as needed.

This technique can help during the evaluation process, and the approach is equally appropriate following an informal drop-in visit. If we are in classrooms on a regular basis, even daily, this lowers the level of concern of the staff member being observed. If I have been in someone's classroom a couple of dozen times, that teacher is much less likely to be uncomfortable during a formal observation visit. This is especially true if I often follow my drop-in-visits with a dialogue that revolves around instruction and, as often as appropriate, is positive in nature.

Using an appropriate approach is also essential in note-taking when observing a teacher. Making judgments such as "poor management" or "needs better control of the class" will often result in a confrontation with the teacher. Not only is morale affected, but more importantly, the teacher will resist efforts for improvement. However, if your notes are more factual, then this sets the stage for a more meaningful dialogue. Instead of judgments, use statements like "9:17 three students had their heads on their desks," "9:28 four boys were at the pencil sharpener pushing each other," or "10:03 three girls were talking loudly in the back of the room during independent practice time."

Documenting the specific behaviors you observed and when they occurred can allow for more neutral, growth-oriented dialogue in the post-visit conference. It is important that you use the same note-taking approach with all staff members so that there is the perception of consistency when you do a formal observation in a classroom.

Sharing these notes with the staff member prior to the post-conference can give them time to reflect on the class. Then asking the member, "Tell me a little bit about…the incidents in the class," can allow for a more productive evaluation session. Though there are times when we need to be very directive, if we can avoid those by providing opportunities for the staff member to self-reflect, it can provide a much more positive growth experience.

THE PROFESSIONAL DEVELOPMENT PLAN— A TOOL FOR POSITIVE GROWTH

One common tool in many school districts is the required development of an individual growth plan, sometimes called a Professional Development Plan (PDP). The PDP includes a goal or objective the teacher wants to achieve and the appropriate procedures for achieving the goal. Do not make the goal cumbersome for the teacher. Stick to one goal and encourage very doable procedures for achieving the goal. We want a PDP to be a natural growth plan, not an additional task in a teacher's very busy world. Most teachers will see that they do this anyway. This process just provides the design of a concrete path to follow and the addition of the principal for support.

The PDP should be written by you and each staff member together. This makes you aware of their focus and direction. You are a resource, providing them with ideas of how they can achieve their goal. You become a part of their professional growth in a very direct, supportive, and influential way. They see how much you care about them individually and the lengths you are willing to go to see them grow professionally.

A way for the leader to effectively time-manage these PDP visits with teachers is actually very simple. Any time you meet with a teacher about their Professional Development Plan, set a date for your next meeting. This way it does not slip your mind and get moved to the back burner, which can be very deflating to a staff member and can be seen as a personal insult to a teacher. Instead, as your meeting draws to a close, say, "When should we get together and touch base on your progress?" And, no matter what, set a future date. If you choose January 15th and that turns out to be too early for a follow-up contact, then at least both of you have that reminder in your calendars. Then, on or before January 15th, reschedule the date so that both of you will be able to keep a focus on the PDP.

An example of this PDP process might begin with a teacher

who wants to learn more about and implement Guided Reading in the classroom. The principal and the teacher would sit down and articulate this goal (objective). Then the fun begins. The two of you brainstorm the ways the teacher can achieve this goal. You discuss books and articles to read, workshops to attend, classroom observations of teachers practicing Guided Reading, or possible college classes that would be applicable. These discussions are always exciting and can get the teacher motivated to achieve the designated goal.

Periodically throughout the year, the teacher should give you feedback on how the PDP is progressing. This can be formal or informal. It might be just a brief conversation on the way to lunch, or a written update for your files. If the plan is followed, you will begin to notice the pride and enthusiasm in the teacher. We all know that knowledge is power. Teachers who are learning continuously begin to empower themselves with their new knowledge, and this leads to better instruction in the classroom. You will encourage these teachers to share the excitement with other faculty, perhaps at a faculty meeting or grade-level meeting. At the end of the year, sit down with all faculty members and celebrate their progress! Some teachers will complete their PDP, while others might ask to extend it over the summer or into the next school year. Evaluate together where they are in the process. Success breeds success. If the PDP has been worth their while, designing the next one will be an invigorating experience for both the principal and the teacher.

Many principals design their own PDP and share it with the faculty before school starts. They can design it based upon feedback from staff and their own personal growth interests. Sharing this with the staff sends the message that you care about growing professionally and you're willing to do the same things you want the staff to do. Being the professional role model is your ultimate job as a principal.

I always kept the PDP template on my computer so the teacher and I could sit down together and create the document right at the computer. A sample PDP format is provided in Figure 5. Your informal conversations and classroom visits can help provide insights into designing the PDP with your teacher. This is a concrete approach enabling each of your teachers to feel as

FIGURE 5

Professional Development Plan

Teacher _____

School _____

Professional Development Goal:

    (state the desired goal/outcome to be accomplished)

Procedures for Achieving Goal:

    (provide specific statements which describe what the teacher is to do to achieve the goal and what the supervisor will do to assist. This is the process, the steps, and the ingredients for change.)

Evaluation/Assessment Method(s) and Date(s):

    (How will we know when progress is made? How will we monitor that progress? What are the short term and long term target dates?)

Comments:

Plan Developed: _____
                       Teacher's Signature/Date

                     _____
                     Supervisor's Signature/Date

If plan revised (Date/Initials): _____

Plan Achieved: _____
                     Teacher's Signature/Date

                     _____
                     Supervisor's Signature/Date

Signatures indicate the document has been read and discussed.
Copies to teacher and supervisor.

though they have a personal and professional goal to attain that feeds into the vision of the school.

BUILD CREDIBILITY FIRST

Regularly reinforcing staff members through notes, positive comments, and the Friday Focus can make them much more willing to accept your ideas and suggestions. (After all, if you have complimented me several times, you must have something going for you!) Setting this positive tone can help establish credibility which can carry us through less positive situations. Teachers, just like parents, are more likely to accept "less than good news" if we provide them with as many positively reinforcing opportunities as possible before we offer suggestions for growth.

Having regular drop-in visits can also allow the focus on the evaluation process to be diminished. It can change the process of instructional improvement from being an "event" to something much richer and an ongoing process. The leader who is in classrooms regularly not only sees teachers in a more natural and relaxed state, but also allows students to be more comfortable and natural in their behavior. Frequent visits also reduce the chance of catching a teacher only on an "off day." Regularly observing our staff members' behaviors can greatly diminish the potential tension and awkwardness that may accompany the formal observation and evaluation process.

The evaluation process may not be viewed as a positive by many staff members. It is essential that it never be a deflating experience, especially for those teachers we are hoping to reinforce. Being aware of how our staff members view the evaluation process is a key first step for turning painful into positive.

PART 4

MEETINGS, MEETINGS, MEETINGS . . . YOU MEAN THESE CAN BE FUN?

10

THE MONTHLY
STAFF MEETING: FROM
DRAB TO DYNAMITE

Monthly staff meetings can be uplifting and effective or they can be boring and unproductive. In the study of more effective and less effective principals described in Chapter 7, according to M. E. Whitaker (1997), "in more effective schools, teachers looked forward to and valued faculty meetings. The converse was true in the less effective schools." One of the most important aspects of this part of the study is the realization that it truly is *possible* to have meetings that staff members look forward to and value!

Making the meetings you facilitate exciting, informative, and productive is essential to the success of your school and to the enhancement of positive staff morale. Everyone on the staff is there, and these opportunities are very precious. In addition, school-wide meetings can help set a tone that can then infiltrate every facet of the mindset of the faculty. If the measure of a truly great movie is that you look at the world in a little different light when you leave, then the measure of a great faculty meeting is that you look at your students and your profession in a more positive light when you leave the meeting. Strategies to ensure that your staff meetings are great should be practiced continuously. The following are ideas that will move your staff meetings from good to great!

Keep Topics and Issues That Can Be Handled in Writing Out of the Meeting

Everyone's time is precious, but the opportunity to be together as a group is invaluable. Because of this, we cannot afford to waste this time dealing with logistics and other less meaningful events. Meetings can get bogged down in discussing upcoming events and dates that can be sent out through a memo (an example of a weekly memo is outlined in Chapter 6). This meeting format creates a one-way discussion that eliminates quality interaction. For instance, do not discuss dates of the next PTA meeting or an upcoming assembly, but do discuss if you want staff participation during either of those.

Build an Agenda with the Staff

The best way to develop the agenda is to gather input from the staff. This is an important way for the staff to see that their input is crucial to the success of the meeting and the organization. In order to gather staff input, have an idea/suggestion box or sheet in a central location accessible to the faculty. Then respond to these ideas by addressing them at the faculty meeting or at other appropriate times, such as grade-level meetings, individual meetings, and professional development meetings. For example, if the staff is concerned about the safety of students as they go to the buses at the end of the day, make sure to have that topic on the next meeting's agenda. If an idea cannot be addressed because of time constraints, be sure to acknowledge this and then make sure you address it at another meeting.

Make Sure That the Discussion Affects Most of the Staff, Most of the Time

Many staff meetings tend to be reduced to a small-group discussion because a certain topic only affects a few people. An example might be discussing specific details about the science curriculum when most of the staff are not science teachers. Small-group meetings, such as departmental meetings, can take care of this. A more productive approach to this situation may be to have the science teachers give a five-minute presentation to the rest of the staff on their curriculum and how it can be integrated with other subjects throughout the school.

FUN AND PRODUCTIVE MEETINGS

The following are more suggestions that can assist with facilitating a valuable and enjoyable meeting.

Stick to the agenda and timeline. This provides continuity and easy understanding of the structure of the meeting. It is important for people to have an idea of what to expect. This directs the focus of the meeting and keeps everyone on the same page. We have all been to meetings and inservices that did not have direction. This gives us the idea that the meeting was not planned out thoroughly; therefore, we feel it is not important. This is not to say that meetings should not capitalize on "teachable moments" when they arise, but the focus or theme of the meeting needs to stay on track.

The following is an example of a meeting that did not stick to the agenda and was very discouraging for me. The meeting was a district-level advisory meeting attended by all of the principals of the district. The agenda was given to us a few days before the meeting. One of the items listed was for each of us to have ten minutes to discuss what ideas our faculties had for improving staff development in our district. We then were to turn in all of our ideas and they were to be compiled for us so that we would each receive a list and description of everyone's ideas. When I received the agenda I saw a real opportunity to get staff input so that I could represent our building in a positive way during this upcoming discussion, along with getting ideas from other schools that could help us. I met with our professional development committee to review our plan for the year and to discuss ideas for next year. The committee then gave the updated information to the entire staff to make comments and give suggestions. After receiving the feedback, the professional development committee and I met to finalize the plan. We did all of this in a matter of three days. As you can imagine, this took commitment and time from many people. We all thought it would be worth it, because this was a real opportunity to give our ideas on improving staff development to the district.

I arrived at the district advisory meeting with a plan and

ideas that I felt represented our school. The meeting started on time and we discussed the initial items on the agenda. We then began to discuss our plans. The first principal started—and continued presenting for 30 minutes. Although this principal had some useful ideas, about half of the others had no opportunity to share theirs before the meeting ended. We were told to just hand in our plans and that we would get to them later if we had time. What this meant to me was that I was not able to share our ideas or hear everyone else's. In turn, I did not have a perspective of what everyone was doing. Furthermore, when I returned to my school, I did not have any information to share.

The intention of this project was great, but the way the meeting went made me feel unappreciated; above all, I did not have the opportunity to present our staff input. Another way to have handled that situation might have been to review the agenda with all of us before the meeting started: "Thank you all for being here. I want to quickly review the agenda and remind you that in order to give everyone time to present, we have to stick to the timeline. After everyone presents, if we find that it would be beneficial to set up an additional meeting for further discussion, we will do that." This would have set the tone without potentially causing bad feelings about having to interrupt a long presentation. The first principal might have limited his presentation to the high points of his plan, and if he had to be reminded of the time he would not have taken it personally. This would better provide for a productive and positive meeting without anyone leaving with negative feelings.

Supply food and drink. This may not sound like a big deal, but it is always appreciated. It is a simple way of showing your staff that you value their time and efforts. The type of food depends on the time and length of the meeting. For a one-to-two-hour meeting, keep the foods simple and easy to eat while meeting. For morning meetings, fruit, bagels, juice, and coffee do the trick. Afternoon meetings should include soda and coffee, along with some simple snacks like party mix, fruit, or a few sweets. If the meeting goes over a lunch hour, you can order out pizza or sub sandwiches to compensate for the teachers missing their lunch hour. The point is to have it ready before the meeting and yet not have it be a tremendous burden to get ready. You could also have parents prepare or at least set up the food for the faculty. The meeting is not about the food; the food is to enhance the meeting. I always thought the tougher the content of the meeting, the better the food I would serve. My faculty knew that if they ever came in and there was lobster and prime rib, they were in for an all-nighter! This is just another way you, as the leader, can show your support for your staff.

Always start and finish on a positive note. Start the meeting with an energizer or with a positive perspective-setter. Have someone share a positive experience or describe something uplifting that you recently observed in a classroom or in the school. Establishing a positive tone is essential for every meeting.

Try not to finish on a hurried or negative note. Put the more mundane or controversial topics toward the beginning of the meeting. Then finish your meeting on a positive note. An example may be to congratulate a teacher who has received a grant or a district award. Another example is to read a motivational quote. On the lighter side of things, you or one of the staff might tell a funny story or joke.

Change locations. Have meetings in different locations or in a variety of classrooms. It is amazing how many teachers have never really sat for a period of time in another teacher's room. This idea not only allows for variety, it is also a good way for teachers to "brag" about their own rooms or activities in their classes. This idea can be set up at all levels. Department meetings can rotate within each of the representatives' rooms; district-level administrative meetings can be held in various buildings.

Have different teachers facilitate and present at meetings. An example is to have the teacher whose room you are in talk about why it is arranged the way it is. This allows teachers to "toot their own horn" about what they are doing and why. Another example is for a group of teachers to present ideas they learned at a workshop or a conference.

Another possibility is to ask a different grade level, interdisciplinary team, or department to present each month. This idea can overcome the issue of not being able to get into every teacher's classroom. This gives the teachers of that unit the freedom to decide whose room to meet in. For example, the four first grade teachers may decide that the best place to meet is in the room where the students have displayed their latest writings. This would provide a visual for their presentation on how they address writing in the first grade. You will be amazed at how much the upper-grade teachers will learn from this simple procedure. You'll hear responses like "I had no idea first grade students could do that," and "This is the first time I really looked at all the things on the walls in a first grade room."

The only logistical arrangement you need to make as a leader is to establish the schedule. I suggest making these arrangements with the teachers. For instance, in a middle school, a seventh grade team may want to present in April because that is when they plan to have a culminating activity to celebrate an integrated unit they have developed. The high school history department may be interested in hosting a faculty meeting in October because a class is finishing a unit on Greece that includes several artifacts they want to share. Giving teachers flexibility with this decision takes away from the perception that you are just adding another thing for them to do. It also promotes an attitude of "we are excited about showing and telling our peers about this." As with many things a good leader does, this shows you recognize and respect all of their hard work.

Have a drawing or gag gift to lighten the tone. This might be something as elaborate as a drawing for dinner for two, or as light as dusting off an old 1956 sophomore high-jump trophy and awarding it to a different person each month. You might have a gift certificate hidden under a chair. You can involve the PTA to fund these gifts, or solicit businesses to donate them. You can even go the next step and invite one of the PTA parents to present the award. This is an easy way for the PTA to show support in a non-threatening, pleasant way.

Laugh, laugh, laugh. Laughter is not only fun, but it is good for you and for the morale of your building. To establish this atmosphere, be willing to laugh at yourself. This shows everyone that it is okay not to take yourself too seriously. This also encourages good humor and a light atmosphere. Assign a different teacher each month to bring a joke to the meeting, or have everyone bring their baby pictures, then see if they can guess who each picture is. Keeping the monthly staff meeting enlightening and informing is essential. This is one aspect of great meetings that is often overlooked. Humor is a great stress reliever and also builds trust. Laughing at yourself and with others shows your confidence and honesty.

Set up your meetings in a comfortable, relaxed, and non-threatening setting. Make sure your teachers are comfortable with the arrangements. Do not allow the negative teachers to intimidate or disrupt the meeting. Whitaker (1999) indicates that in many schools, negative staff members can intimidate the rest of the staff during faculty meetings.

It is essential that you address this situation. I have to admit that I have been in charge of meetings and have felt uncomfortable due to a group of negative staff. At times I felt that there was nothing I could do about this other than taking reactive measures, such as talking to them after the meeting about my expectations of staff behavior. What this did was give them even more power; they accomplished their goal of being negative and bringing me down with them. As Whitaker goes on to explain, these negative teachers can turn the positive teachers into the most uncomfortable people at the meeting. We, as the leaders of these staff meetings, must be the ones to change the environmental dynamics of the room.

In many schools, negative staff members with strong personalities have intimidated some of the other faculty. In addition, the principal is often uncomfortable with or at times even unnerved by these people. This discomfort or intimidation is not pleasant, but the principal who keeps it in mind can easily imagine how the other teachers and staff in the school feel.

Where do difficult teachers often sit at faculty meetings? When hundreds of groups of school administrators were asked this question, three responses consistently arose: the difficult people sit *together, in the back,* and *near the door.* If any or all of these three patterns are true in your school, then ask yourself, "Who are the most comfortable people in the room?"

Think of attending church on Sunday. Which rows fill up first? Often, it's the back rows. When I became principal of a school with several challenging staff members, we did not have one table of malcontents—they had to push several tables together. I thought, "If I am uncomfortable at staff meetings, how do my good teachers feel?" Historically, most teacher comments at the staff meetings were negative, and the positive members seldom contributed. I knew I had to address this problem. I will explain how I did it shortly. However, I would like to take you through a scenario first.

Let us say that at a faculty meeting, some staff members are expressing concerns about student discipline and/or behavior. One of your superstars, sitting in the middle of the room or toward the front, raises her hand and says, "I think we should start a lunch detention program. We could use an empty classroom near the cafeteria and kids who have not behaved appropriately at school could eat their lunch in that room to take away the social element for a day. It would be immediate, we would not have to worry about transportation before or after school with the students, and taking them away from their peers is very effective." Then she adds, "We could easily do this if every staff member volunteered to give up their lunch hour one day a month to supervise this lunch detention room."

What would be the reaction from the back of the room, where your difficult teachers were sitting together? There would be moaning, laughing, or maybe even sarcastic comments, such as "You look like you need to give up lunch!" The real question is, who is the least comfortable person in the room at this time? Your superstar is—and this has to change. Your superstars' morale is too essential to let it be affected in this manner. The other result of such an incident is its effect on your new faculty members. If I am a new teacher, what did I just learn? I discovered that at faculty meetings, I should either be quiet or say negative things. This does not benefit anyone's perspective in a positive way.

As the principal faced with difficult people sitting at faculty meetings together, in the back, and near the door, I realized that if the dynamics within our staff meeting were going to be different, it was up to me to alter them. Traditionally, our staff meetings were held in the media center/library, using the random table arrangement that was in place for the school day. There were many more chairs than there were staff members. Thus, not only did the more negative people sit in the back, everyone was very spread out over quite a physical distance. I quickly realized that I was going to be uncomfortable in these staff meetings. And if I, the principal, was uncomfortable, what were the other teachers feeling?

One other thing that I noticed was that even though most people would prefer to sit in the back row at a meeting, and my most difficult people arrived at the meeting last, the other more positive teachers would not take their chairs. It was as if these seats were emotionally "saved" for these negative staff members. Now that was informal power. How to alter these dynamics?

After putting much thought into it, I decided to rearrange the media center just before each staff meeting. We turned the chairs and tables around so that the traditional back was the front and the front was the back. We also removed all the extra chairs, to establish as much physical closeness as possible. Finally, the chairs were arranged in an opera-house style, with each chair facing the front. Generally, the most difficult people come in last. With this new arrangement, the difficult people did not have their "reserved" section; now, as other staff members entered the room, they filled the chairs starting in the back. Then as the more negative staff filed into the room, the only seats open were right down front. Now the more negative folks are sitting in the front of the room, and they are the most uncomfortable people in the room. Then, in keeping with my non-confrontational style, at the start of the meeting I said with a genuine smile on my face, "Isn't it neat to have change once in a while? I thought we could give this arrangement a try." It was amazing how taking negative faculty out of their comfort zone caused them to be much quieter and less willing to voice their often confrontational opinions in staff meetings.

After a couple of meetings, I once again reversed the room from back to front and front to back, but I left it in the opera-house style and continued to remove all of the extra tables and chairs. However, I permanently eliminated the two back tables that had once been the domain of the negative staff. I pushed the two tables together, took away the chairs from around them, and put the cookies, snacks, and beverages on the tables. After all, shouldn't the food be near the door?

One final strategy: At staff meetings I would have my assistant principal come into the room last. He would sit next to our most vocal negative staff member, very nicely asking, "Is this seat taken?" The negative person now becomes the most uncomfortable person in the room, and also the least likely to make negative comments at the meeting.

Ironically, as principal we would not think twice about sitting next to a positive teacher at a meeting, but we feel uncomfortable about sitting beside our most negative faculty. This is another example of how we often give informal power to our most difficult teachers. And when other staff members are present, they observe this dynamic also. Taking away that power and making the difficult people uncomfortable is very important in developing the culture of the school. Faculty meetings are an important and visible part of that process.

Faculty meetings also provide an opportunity for the principal to model how to work appropriately with difficult teachers. The approach we take with difficult staff members will demonstrate to the rest of the faculty how to remain in control and how to avoid arguments and power struggles. This will be a valuable tool for the positive staff members to observe. It will allow others in the school to use these effective strategies with their negative peers.

Focusing on transferring the power and comfort levels from the negative staff to the positive effective staff can enhance staff meetings greatly. In addition, transferring this power models your expectations and priorities, which are to make your organization as effective as possible.

Set up meetings with different formats. Many schools have staff meetings twice a month. One idea that can allow you to take advantage of this opportunity is to have one meeting be traditional and the other be in a format of reflection. These "forums" can be a great way to enhance staff communication and reflection. This gives your staff the most valuable gift of all—time! Time for reflection and discussion can not only improve communication and instruction strategies, but also be a great way to rejuvenate and reenergize.

You can begin initial discussions about alternatives to traditional meetings by getting feedback on how the faculty feels about the current structure of your meetings. From this beginning, possible topics can be received through a suggestion folder. Putting the forum discussion on the agenda of a regular staff meeting is the next step. Topics can range from curriculum, to professional growth, to a discussion based on an article or book.

Providing different formats can stimulate discussion from faculty, increase faculty involvement, and provide variety. I have been involved with forums that are very effective if the topics are developed and directed by staff. For example, in an elementary school the teachers wanted to discuss effective literacy-block teaching strategies. Instead of having one or two people set up a presentation, it was agreed that everyone would bring at least one example of what they do in their literacy block that had been successful. It was also okay to bring examples of what had not been effective. What resulted was that not only did the most effective and confident teachers bring great examples, but they also shared their ideas that were not as successful. This format took pressure off the teachers who were not sure what to present. The format also encouraged all members to be at an equal level, which promoted open and relaxed discussion. Finally, this format allowed teachers to "celebrate" and "honor" their own accomplishments, as well as each other's! This made for an eventful and informative meeting with a wonderful atmosphere.

Make your holiday meeting extra special. One of my favorite things is to take advantage of the atmosphere that accompanies the holiday season by doing something extra special at the December staff meeting. I would usually have one of my custodians, dressed in my personal Santa Claus suit, come Ho-Ho-Ho-ing into the meeting with gifts for everyone on the staff. It might be a new staff T-shirt, a monogrammed mouse pad, or personalized business cards for everyone. This was the ideal time of the year to "go begging" to a local business to provide these for our school employees.

Additionally, I would read a special story. It might be the classic "Three Letters From Teddy," or the Chris Van Allsburg book *The Polar Express*. Even my high school faculty loved it each year. Or, you could set the tone of the meeting by asking everyone to share their favorite holiday memory. Taking advantage of this emotional time of the year can be very helpful to boost staff morale during a high-stress period.

Finally, set up a way to get *feedback* on your meetings. Surveys, suggestion boxes, and informal visits are a few ways to obtain feedback. The information you can gain from suggestion boxes can be very enlightening. Many people who may not be very verbal in meetings love the chance to be able to make com-

ments in writing. I will never forget the time I received a suggestion from a very positive teacher about making sure the meetings include everybody, not just the outspoken teachers. She gave
the example of how one teacher from the social studies department talked on the topic of what grade levels should teach eco-
nomics and why. She said that I took that comment as a
representation from the entire department, which I did. This
teacher asserted that these comments *did not* represent everyone. I was very surprised by this note, because the teacher who
spoke at the staff meeting and the teacher who wrote the note
were best friends. I had assumed that they had the same views,
when indeed that was not the case.

Surveys are another way to obtain feedback. The power of
surveys is discussed in Chapter 7. Surveys allow teachers to make
comments and respond to questions about staff meetings. This
is how ideas such as forums, increased reflection time, and
teacher-directed meetings can come about.

Informal visits are a very important source of feedback. As
an effective leader you need to solicit information from teachers. One way to do this is to be "out and about." This provides
more opportunities for teachers to talk to you in informal settings. When you are out where the action is, it is easier to approach teachers in a non-threatening way to ask for feedback.
For example, while you are on hall duty you could ask, "Mrs.
Johnson, did the plan to address our diversity project make sense
to you?" This gives Mrs. Johnson an opening to talk about her
ideas in a relaxed setting.

The most important point to gain from this feedback is a
perspective of what teachers are thinking and feeling about the
staff meetings. These strategies not only show teachers that you
value their thoughts, but also can lead to more productive and
enjoyable meetings.

The monthly meeting can be drab or dynamite; you can make
meetings mediocre or fantastic. Being conscious of what people
feel about the meetings, trying new things, and focusing on improving will make you and your staff actually look forward to
these meetings.

11

SMALL-GROUP MEETINGS

A lack of time is one of the greatest concerns of people in all organizations. Too many meetings is one aspect contributing to this lack of time. Educators are no exception to this phenomenon. Increased expectations, deadlines, at-risk students, and test scores are all factors that elevate the stress level of teachers. Because of this, we, as leaders, need to keep meetings to a minimum. When we do conduct meetings, they should be as productive, efficient, meaningful, and enjoyable as possible. This chapter will discuss how small-group meetings, both formal and informal, can increase participation and input throughout the organization, and allow a maximum number of people to be involved in the decision-making process.

TIPS FOR PRODUCTIVE GROUPS

Small-group meetings are important for the success of any organization. Because they can take up an enormous amount of time, it is very important to keep them productive and positive. There are several keys to facilitating quality small-group meetings. A top priority is to have all involved **feel valued**. This promotes a sense of importance that allows each person to make sincere and helpful contributions to the meeting.

The first aspect to look at when planning a small-group meeting is to **evaluate the reason** for the meeting. There may be times that after this initial evaluation you realize you can accomplish your goals and objectives without the meeting. The next aspect of meeting planning is determining **who** needs to attend. Giving the staff as much flexibility in attending as possible encourages participation and shows your support. An example of this is asking for one voluntary representative from each grade level, team, or department to attend, instead of asking specific individuals. It is helpful to keep a journal of who attends each meeting and the outcomes that are achieved. This will show you if the same people are doing all the work, as well as showing you if some staff members are not taking part in the decision-making process.

When you are in the development phase of the meeting, get the staff involved in the planning process. For example, instead of saying "We need a budget committee," you can initiate the conversation by **outlining the objectives** and procedures of the committee. The staff can than give their input on how they want to participate. They might just want you to come back to them at a later date when the budget is further along, rather than actually help plan the budget. This shows their trust in you and also indicates to you that their interest level might not be as high as you initially thought.

After defining the objective of the meeting and establishing its participants, it is time to set up the meeting. Deciding **where** to have the meeting and **how long** it should last are important. This all sounds as if it takes a lot of time, but for monthly meetings it becomes more of an expectation or habit than extra work. For example, consider monthly grade-level meetings. At the beginning of the year, the preliminary discussion should address what the meetings are for and who needs to participate. For instance, in many buildings these meetings are held in the teachers' classrooms and are at specific times in order to accommodate the teachers' personal and professional time constraints.

Examples of more formal meetings include leadership teams, administrative advisory councils, and instructional improvement councils. Less formal groups might include grade-level or department teams, specific teams, or even informal visits. As you can see, the titles of these groups indicate collective decision making. As the leader, you need to make sure the groups' decision-making approach is inclusive. The title should indicate the "mission" of the group. If the group is described as "advisory," you need to make sure you take the advisement to heart and act on it. If you cannot carry out the advisement, you need to let the group know why and what other possibilities are available. The knowledge of how to set up small-group meetings is essential. The following are examples of ideas for small-group meetings— both formal and informal—that have been successful in schools.

FORMAL LEADERSHIP ROLES

There has been much discussion of the roles of teachers in more formal leadership positions (Berry and Ginsberg 1990; Darling-Hammond and Berry 1988). These roles include department chairs, members of principal advisory councils, team leaders, grade-level coordinators, and structured committee chairs. These positions play important roles in a child-centered school. Being sensitive to who the informal leaders are in a school and linking them with the formal leadership roles is an important element in developing staff leadership.

In 1989, Ralph Tyler discussed the importance of the principal's leadership in promoting student learning. His findings reported that schools with substantial improvements in students' learning accomplished this by cooperative efforts of teachers, parents, and other interested community members. Schools worked together with these involved parties to identify and develop solutions for significant educational problems. This team approach to problem solving requires a shared understanding and commitment to mission. The principal must make sure all parties are well grounded in the school's purpose and goals. The principal must then help the team focus on the significant problems as identified by the teachers.

After the problem is identified, a solution must be developed. There is rarely only one solution to most educational problems. The team needs to look at all possible solutions and choose the one that presents itself as the most effective and feasible. The team must then implement this solution and answer the following questions:

1. What present school practices will need to be changed?

2. What changes in the curriculum are necessary?

3. What new teaching procedures will need to be used?

4. How will the teachers involved gain the skills required to employ these teaching procedures successfully?

5. What new instructional materials are needed and how can they be obtained or constructed?

6. What changes are required in the daily and weekly school schedule?

These questions require deliberative thought and an appropriate schedule for implementation. The team should not expect too much too soon and they should make the schedule realistic. Transforming people's beliefs and skills takes time and patience. Effective problem solving is one of the primary tasks of today's administrator.

Howes and McCarthy (1982) described how a team approach to participative management was organized in a New York school district and its schools. At the building level, a cabinet consisted of five to twelve members and included all administrators and representative teachers. The cabinet was assigned several primary responsibilities:

1. Review school budget proposals and make recommendations.

2. Develop student discipline policy.

3. Provide input to the design of the master schedule.

4. Review student evaluation procedures.

5. Assist in the recruiting and training of staff.

6. Develop a co-curricular program.

7. Develop plans regarding school climate.

8. Develop a community relations program.

9. Establish school goals and priorities (p. 5).

The results from going to a participatory team were very positive. This was indicated by both team members and non-team members. Surveys from faculty about the district-level participative management structure indicated that both groups perceived it to be a positive process. The team members indicated to Howes and McCarthy:

1. Persons affected by decisions were generally involved in them.
2. School/district goals were emphasized in reaching decisions.
3. Team members understood their roles.
4. The team to some extent was an effective decision maker, problem solver and handler of routing decisions.
5. The team work was limited in its influence on district activities.
6. The team did not emphasize subject-area micro-goals in reaching decisions.
7. The different teams did not plan together or coordinate their activities.

Perhaps even more significant, the non-team members indicated many positive responses to the team development:

1. The teams did provide staff with information necessary to perform their jobs.
2. Team members were receptive to staff ideas and suggestions.
3. The teams provided staff with information on decisions that affected them.
4. The implementation of the team concept increased staff participation in decision making, provided necessary leadership for school/district operations, and contributed to the motivation of personnel.

Kritek (1986) examined the literature involving school culture as an aspect of participative management. He indicated that a school's success may be influenced by the "structure that provides a sense of commitment and identity for the staff" (p. 10). Staff participation and input are two of the concepts Kritek stated could help enhance this positive school culture.

The level of formality of participatory management committees, councils, and teams differs greatly among schools. In *High School Leaders and Their Schools, Volume II: Profiles of Effectiveness,* Pellicer, Anderson, Keefe, Kelley, and McCleary, (1990) observed that most research on participative management has been done on the district rather than the school level. The authors examined the administrative teams in a sampling of schools. They found:

The administrative team always included the assistant principal(s), and often other key staff members such as a counselor, a department chair, a teacher representative or union building representative, or the director of activities or athletics. (In the larger schools of 1400 students or more, an assistant principal was directly responsible for counseling services or activities/athletics.) Additional teachers, usually elected, sometimes were members. Size and composition of the administrative team appeared to be directly related to constituencies and followed the management principle of functional representation (pp. 18–19).

Two factors that affected the team operation were the degree of formal status accorded the team and the extent of delegation of authority. Some teams operated without the principal and with no agenda. Others were scheduled weekly or biweekly and had a much more structured format (Pellicer et al. 1990).

The structures and programs that involve and/or promote participative management are many and varied. Garten and Valentine (1989) suggest the development of two types of management committees. The first is the Administrative Advisory Council (AAC).

ADMINISTRATIVE ADVISORY COUNCIL

The purpose of the AAC is described as follows:
The AAC is designed to allow for faculty input into the daily

operations of the school. Following is a typical statement of purpose for this type of committee: "Throughout the school, numerous problems arise that have implications for the professional staff members and the overall school program. The AAC functions so that the thoughts of the professional staff members may be adequately and clearly expressed to the administration" (p. 4).

Garten and Valentine described six responsibilities of the AAC:

1. Determine the feelings of the staff members about managerial/procedural issues through discussions with staff members and surveys of their attitudes about specific issues.

2. Interpret the feelings and view of the staff members to the administration on a regular basis.

3. Make specific recommendations to the administration regarding significant concerns.

4. Assist the administration, as appropriate, in the resolution of problems and concerns.

5. Conduct an annual "school climate survey," including but not limited to management and procedural issues.

6. Assist the administration in identifying school goals (p. 4).

Garten and Valentine suggested that the committee be made up of five to twelve faculty members, depending on the size of the teaching staff. The committee should meet without the administration; then the chairperson, or the committee as a whole, should meet with the principal to discuss issues.

INSTRUCTIONAL IMPROVEMENT COUNCIL

The second building-level committee Garten and Valentine proposed is the Instructional Improvement Council (IIC). The purpose of the IIC is described as follows:

The IIC provides faculty input into the curricular and instructional aspects of the school. A typical statement of purpose for this type of committee might be: "The IIC provides for coordination, facilitation, and evaluation of the ongoing curricular and instructional program in order to ensure the most effective instructional environment for students" (p. 5).

Garten and Valentine provided examples of the responsibilities of the IIC:

1. Determine the inservice needs of the faculty members; make recommendations for the development of appropriate programs to meet those needs; assist in planning and implementing such programs.

2. Assess curricular needs; evaluate current curricular offerings and proposed curricular changes; make recommendations regarding curricular programs.

3. Review current instructional-level objectives and make recommendations regarding changes and evaluation procedures.

4. Analyze student achievement on criterion-referenced and standardized tests; make recommendations for program improvement as appropriate.

5. Review supervisory and evaluative procedures and needs; make recommendations for change as appropriate (pp. 5–6).

According to Garten and Valentine, the IIC committee should consist of representatives of the faculty by instructional division (grade levels, teams, or departments), the instructional media center, and the counseling staff. An administrator should not be a committee member, but should be an ex-officio member (attend the meetings, provide input, but not vote).

Another formal leadership structure is the leadership team. It combines many of the aspects of the administrative advisory council with those of the instructional improvement council.

THE LEADERSHIP TEAM

Leadership teams are essential to the success of the school. They can be set up in several different ways. The objective of the leadership team is to provide direction for the school and promote collaboration among the entire staff. These teams cover topics such as professional development planning, cross-grade learning activities, and curriculum development. As the leader, you may or may not facilitate this team. But the most important factor is that you are an **equal** in the group. Many leadership teams in schools report their work to the staff and principal, with the principal not being the facilitator of the group. An example may be that the team is looking at and planning cross-grade activities for the school. They will report and update the staff with ideas they have generated. You, as principal, should already have had input with logistics such as the schedule, but you do not direct the team. The fact that the team is researching possible ideas and is communicating with the staff will increase ownership and collaboration. People selected to a leadership team should be the people that will most be affected by their decisions and recommendations. For instance, in a cross-grade activity team, representation from classroom teachers, special education teachers, as well as administrators should be a part of the group. At times the group may even bring in custodians, food service employees, and other non-teaching staff, depending on whether they are affected by decisions made by the group.

Having representation from different departments of the school is essential for a successful leadership team. This group can be set up according to academic department, grade level, or teams. These team meetings can be scheduled monthly or bimonthly. Topics may include budget, professional development ideas, staff meeting agendas and structure, as well as suggestions for school-wide positive reinforcement tactics. The topics are ones that have an impact on the entire school. These teams can also provide an avenue of two-way communication for the entire staff.

Though the principal is ultimately responsible for everything that takes place in a school, involving faculty in the decision-making process is crucial in allowing the effective implementation of new programs, curriculum, or any type of change in a building. The leadership team can function under many names: Principal's Advisory Committee, Principal's Council, Administrative Committee, Leadership Team, and the like. The membership of the leadership team is crucial to its success. Included on the team should/could be representatives from each team (or grade level depending on school size and desire), members from the exploratory area and special education, guidance counselor, media specialist, assistant principal(s), and the principal. Non-certificated staff could be included. Other schools include the student council sponsor, activity coordinator, department coordinators, or any additional staff members that are appropriate.

These are the official positions on the committee, but an examination of the members of the committee is essential in determining the membership. Team selection criteria should take into consideration several areas:

- ◆ Diversity—representation based on age, gender, race, and so forth.

- ◆ Time commitment—for meeting attendance, reporting to other staff members, and attending any training needed for committee members.

- ◆ Credibility with the rest of the faculty—It is critical that the informal leaders of the school be on the committee so that the committee's decisions will be effectively accepted by the school as a whole.

- ◆ Openness to learning—The leadership team committee members have to be open to new ideas and concepts.

- ◆ Effective communicators—The leadership team members must be able to listen to the views of other committee members and to the faculty they represent. They must also be able to share with the group both their views and opinions and those of other staff members who are not on the committee.

- ◆ Whole-school perspective—Though all committee members have their own views and interests, the more ability they have to envision how decisions affect the entire school, the more they will be able to make valuable, informed contributions to the leadership team and school.

♦ Teacher organization representation—The committee must also be able to effectively communicate with and represent the teachers' organizations or unions that impact the school and district decision making.

In reference to implementing change, Stevens (1990) concludes that the proper climate is necessary for successful school reformation. The first steps taken by the staff and principal must be non-threatening. Informal discussion with key staff members or school improvement teams with building representatives could be a possible first step. Long-term improvement is possible through staff commitment. The staff must be made aware of current research in the area of reform and understand how this supports the implementation of change within the school. This exposure to research should be ongoing and coupled with continuing dialogue on improvement issues. Staff members should be sent to timely workshops and conferences that pertain to the reform area. Successful change must also include stability in leadership and a realistic timeline for the school improvement project.

It is also critical that the leadership team will be a positive influence on the school. One way that this can be done is by examining the informal leadership within the team before establishing exactly who is a part of it, and ensuring that the informal leaders and positive influences in the faculty are included. An example of this would be a school that has a very positive and influential teacher leader who is not in a role that we might think of as being on the team. In that case, determine a way that they would be included; in other words, either make sure that they get in a role that would allow them to be a part of the leadership team or make sure that a role they currently play is included. A principal could have the assistant student council sponsor included if the faculty member who is in that role should be a part of the committee. During the initial formulation of the leadership team structure, it is essential to consider the makeup of the committee and the probable tone that the members bring to meetings through their personalities.

The leadership team should meet regularly as well as at additional times if needed. Some schools have the teams meet the

Monday before a Wednesday faculty meeting, for example, so that they can go over any agenda items beforehand and present other issues that may be appropriate. It is also critical that the leadership team be the resolving influence for most issues that it raises. To have the committee bring problems to the principal and the principal be expected to resolve them alone is not the purpose of the group.

Principal Advisory Teams

Many aspects of a principal's advisory team are similar to leadership teams. The difference is that this team provides direction and ideas for the principal. If you are in a small school, this team can include your entire staff. In a larger school, this team may consist of department or grade-level representatives. This group not only is a great way to promote communication and collaboration, but also can assist the principal by representing the school at district and state meetings when appropriate. Giving staff feedback from district administrators' meetings provides a feeling of "being in the know" for this selected staff. These meetings are most effective if scheduled on a regular basis so teachers can arrange their calendars in advance. If possible, have the team members themselves set the dates and times of the meetings.

Informal Groups

Though it may be necessary to have one or more of the pre-viously-mentioned formal leadership groups in a school, no school can exist without many informal committees or groups. Having the informal groups function efficiently and effectively is a critical aspect of staff satisfaction and morale. Let's take a look at some of these more informal teams and groups.

Specific-Purpose Teams

These teams should be kept to a minimum, but they are essential to the communication, trust, and productivity of the school. Examples of possible headings for these teams include budget, professional development, and cross grade/academic area. The principal is a part of these teams, but not the leader. Many of these meetings do not even have to be attended by the principal! This shows trust from the principal and may increase staff morale. These groups should initiate self-directed deadlines in order to promote efficiency and productivity.

GRADE-LEVEL TEAMS

These monthly meetings may be one of the best ways to promote communication and support between principal and staff. These meetings discuss everything from curriculum issues to parent issues to standardized tests. The most important role of the principal in these meetings is to **listen.** These meetings allow teachers an avenue to discuss any issue they feel is relevant at the time. This is also a great time to get input on how the team is thinking about other groups, such as the office professionals, special education support, luncheon staff, and custodians.

These meetings should include every group in the building. Meeting monthly with custodians, cafeteria people, bus drivers, office professionals, and non-homeroom staff not only shows their importance, but can provide you with information that is valuable to the entire staff.

TEACHER-INITIATED AND DIRECTED MEETINGS

These meetings could be based around traditional topics such as teaching strategies. They also can be activities such as dialogue groups to discuss books, or get-togethers at a home or lounge after school. The most important ingredient for the success of these meetings is that they are truly staff-initiated and directed.

INFORMAL VISITS

Small-group meetings are very valuable, but they should not restrict communication at other times. For instance, a staff that knows they can visit with you at any time is a staff that feels listened to. The staff members should feel that they do not have to wait for the next meeting if they think an issue or problem needs to be addressed right away. Informal or impromptu visits and meetings are *very important*. They allow you not only to put out fires, but, at times, to stop them before they start.

Small-group meetings are essential and can add a great deal to schools. They can allow for and promote staff communication, provide an avenue for you to show your support to your staff, and spread the responsibility of having a great school throughout the entire staff. They also are more personal, which increases the chances for everyone to participate. The last point is to keep them as fun as possible. They can be great ways to increase staff morale!

12

OPPORTUNITIES FOR RENEWAL

As a school leader, you are often the creator and organizer of staff gatherings that are not faculty meetings. Retreats, inservices, study groups, and social gatherings provide occasions to assemble the staff in creative settings. These times together offer a unique opportunity to renew, educate, and energize faculty. This can have a direct effect on staff morale. If people enjoy and learn from professional growth opportunities, they will be happier returning to the classroom and more willing to try something new. This willingness to explore possibilities can lead to future teaching success, surrounded by the good feeling from the staff development inservice or retreat.

Most meetings follow a familiar routine: participants arrive, they are involved in the workshop event, and they leave. Sometimes invitations are sent in advance, and a summary document is sent following the meeting. All of these seemingly "dry" meeting elements offer you the opportunity to make the occasion special and worth remembering. This chapter will provide ideas to stimulate and invigorate your next staff gathering, thus improving staff morale.

RETREATS AND INSERVICES

Most schools have regular inservice staff development for teachers. These are often half-day workshops, usually in the afternoon when the children have been dismissed at noon. Sometimes they are a full day before school starts, a Saturday during the school year, or a day at the end of the school year. They are even week-long events held during summer months. These full days and weeks are often called retreats because of the length involved. The ideas presented in the following section can be applied to both inservice or retreat events. Modify them to suit your needs and elaborate to add interest to your occasion.

Choose settings that inspire. Often inservices are held in the school itself to keep staff from having to travel if they are already at school. If you choose to stay in the building, give thought to where you will house your meeting. Make sure the chairs are comfortable and there is plenty of table room for teachers to take notes and peruse handouts. The lighting should be appropriate, and avoid crowded spaces if at all possible.

If a full-day retreat is planned, think about trying a location away from school. Removing staff from the all-too-familiar school setting can be enjoyable and motivational to them. They aren't tempted on break to run to the classroom and pick up something or check voice mail or e-mail. There is no intercom disrupting the meeting, or bells ringing to remind them of school functions. When considering alternate locations, be open-minded and creative. Think about your community and some of its important structures. Some ideas include art museums, historic buildings, conference rooms of local corporations, and meeting rooms at country clubs, hotels, or restaurants. If you live in a town that has a college or university, these settings usually offer a variety of options for quality retreat experiences. In addition, local and national parks supply multiple options for giving the staff a unique experience. Besides the obvious variety of meeting locations, many parks have team-building and leadership-training courses. These provide the faculty an opportunity to complete a physical activity course that builds group support and team cohesiveness.

Send inventive invitations. If this is an event you want people to know is special and important, send them invitations. The invitation might be a simple piece of colored paper with information about the event on it. Include graphics or clip art when possible. Think of creative wording enticing them to come to the workshop. A humorous or inspirational quote can catch attention also. Look through books, the Internet, magazines, or even greeting cards to get ideas. If the retreat or event is extremely important or special, consider having invitations printed. Most computers have endless capabilities to print stylish and artistic products on eye-catching paper or correspondence cards. Attaching something to the invitation can also ensure it will get noticed. A crayon pasted to the announcement of an art workshop or a ribbon in school colors attached to your opening faculty meeting notice can catch the readers' attention and give them a sense of your meeting. An invitation also gives the participant something concrete to refer to and keep posted as a reminder. Be creative and imaginative when inviting people to your next gathering.

Make thoughtful arrangements. Take the time to survey the room and furniture available for your event. Are there ways to rearrange the existing format to better suit the needs of your workshop? Do you want people in small groups? Can tables be angled to better view the speaker's location? Are the chairs comfortable for adults to sit in for a period of time? Creating a comfortable and functional room arrangement will be appreciated by participants and create the optimal learning environment for them.

Make sure participants have access to clean and adequate restrooms. Be ready to supply directions as to their location and have someone check them periodically to be sure they are continuously well-maintained.

Provide creature comforts. Creature comforts refer to the things you can do and items you can provide to make participants more comfortable throughout their experience. This is a critical element for any renewal event, but very important for retreats or workshops that last more than a couple of hours.

Greeting people as they enter the workshop is always a positive and professional way to set a pleasant tone for the workshop. This activity takes no money, just your friendly smile and words of welcome. This is especially important for activities where some participants don't know anyone. You can become an immediate connection for them and help them begin to feel comfortable in this new environment. Having background music playing and a welcome greeting on the overhead screen can also add to creating comfort from the start.

Food and snacks are always important features for workshop planners to give close attention. Providing coffee, juice, muffins, and fruit is always a good way to begin a morning workshop. These give people a chance to nourish themselves, interact while eating, and have their familiar cup of morning coffee. Beginning in this fashion helps people settle in for the day and start to feel comfortable. A midmorning snack of fruit and drink can usually help people continue through lunch. If you are providing lunch, make sure you have had detailed conversation with the caterer about numbers needed and the lunch entree. It is important to always have enough food and ensure that a variety of options are available. Keep in mind that some people are vegetarians or may have allergies related to certain foods. A selection of items helps these people make appropriate choices. Afternoon snacks are a must! This can often be the hardest time to keep your audience involved and happy. Popcorn, pretzels, Crackerjacks, fruit, and (of course) something chocolate can keep people nourished and energized. Offer soft drinks, water, and perhaps even coffee or hot chocolate (especially during cold winter months). Also consider keeping a basket or dish of mints, hard candy, and chocolate kisses on each table at all times. This gives participants an edible option when it's not time for a scheduled snack or lunch break.

Be cognizant of room temperature and lighting. Make sure the room is not too hot or too cold. Provide adequate lighting for note-taking and reading of materials. These may seem simple and fundamental, but we have all seen the climate of an event deteriorate quickly due to lack of attention to these elements.

Supply participants with an agenda, handouts, notepads, and pens or pencils. In their hurry to get to a workshop, many people forget these items and are relieved when they are provided. It lowers their level of stress and connects them immediately with workshop content. Often, local businesses or corporations will donate paper and pens for your event.

Door prizes also add an element of fun and excitement to your workshop. These prizes can be items donated or purchased through your budget. Some leaders have also used the free items they get at national conventions in the exhibit halls. Consider these suggestions for educational retreat door prizes: a supply of markers, pens, and pencils; brightly colored packs of Post-It Notes; a selection of colored paper; computer software; books; dinners at local restaurants; gift certificates to a teacher store or bookstore; weekend packages at a local resort; staff T-shirts, mouse pads, or coffee mugs; or a morning at a local spa. The options for door prizes are limited only by your creativity. Many hotels, restaurants, and stores will donate items when they know it will support the local schools.

If possible, have centerpieces for the tables that promote the theme or purpose of your meeting. One high school principal had a spring retreat and provided potted plants on each table. They were given away as door prizes at the end. During a January retreat, another principal had his art students create centerpieces with a snowflake theme. These were especially appreciated as they were a continuous visual reminder of why participants were there . . . in the best interest of students.

Hey, give me a break! Schedule breaks into the workshop or retreat. People need the opportunity to move around, interact, and refresh themselves. Always allow at least 10 to 15 minutes for a break. Any shorter time than this can make participants rush and return feeling that they didn't even have a break. Use this opportunity to play music and have an inspirational quote or humorous cartoon on the overhead screen. When announcing the break, give a sneak preview of the exciting event that will follow the break. Perhaps there will be a door prize drawing, or a surprise—a fun activity, a trinket placed at their seat, or a humorous story or joke.

Also consider getting feedback during the break. I set out Post-It Notes with markers and encourage participants to write one thing they have learned, comments, or questions on these notes during their break. The group then posts these on chart paper, chalkboard, or even available wall space. It provides me with feedback and what needs the audience might have. I can address their questions during the remainder of the workshop.

Facilitate an activity upon the return from a break. This can help people refocus on the content and presentation. It might be a door prize drawing coupled with a reflective writing time to help the audience synthesize what they have learned so far. A human development activity (HDA) is always a good alternative. HDAs are activities that pull the audience back into the content in covert and overt ways. Some examples include group listing of the "Top Ten Things We Have Learned," walking around the room sharing two things you have learned with other workshop members, or a group summary of workshop content on chart paper.

Don't have an identity crisis! Consider supplying name tags for your event if participants don't know each other. According to Feigelson (1998), name tags serve three major purposes:

1. They allow people to address each other by name.

2. They provide additional information about the person that can stimulate conversation and help people make connections.

3. They help elicit a smile and create an inviting, friendly, positive tone (p.32–33).

The author also suggests some creative ways to add information to a name tag that will promote conversation and enjoyment. People are instructed to write their name on their tag and some additional items. The following are her ideas:

♦ *Add the name of someone who makes you laugh.* This can be a writer, movie star, comedian, or someone you know.

♦ *Three numbers that are all significant to you, for any reason at all.* She shares that one administrator put the numbers 3, 1, and 10 on her name badge. Three was the number of grown children she had; one was the number of husbands she had; and ten was how many years it had been since she last cleaned her kitchen "junk" drawer.

♦ *A significant personal or professional first you've had in the past year.* This reflective approach gives participants current information about their peers.

◆ *Three things about me, two of which are true.* This can promote a guessing game regarding which of the three isn't true. It can also foster the discovery of common interests.

◆ *Headlines.* This is to be anything that the person feels is important in their lives. It could relate to something personal or professional. Some examples might be: "Goal Achieved!" "New Grandparent!" "Top of Desk Finally Seen!" "Guess Who Got Married!"

◆ *Something positive about me that people in the room probably can't tell just by looking.* Again, these ideas can be about anything. It is an opportunity to spread good news, share a personal accomplishment, or relate some obscure piece of information. Quality conversation and common interests will evolve from this activity.

◆ *Something I could use help with.* This can generate conversation and potentially solve problems. Requests for help can emerge from home life or professional life. From "Running Toilet" to "Job Leads," this name tag addition ensures lively conversation.

◆ *Something I know quite a bit about.* This gives participants the chance to share their strengths and potentially find resources for future use. Examples include "Web site design," "antique hunting," "playing the piano," "home renovation," or "marathon training."

Keep them active. We are all aware that making human beings sit for long periods of time is not an optimal learning situation. When planning your workshop or retreat, create opportunities for movement and participant involvement. These can range from quick energizer activities to group project assignments during the day. There are many books that provide energizer ideas, and take the time to think about what you have seen outstanding presenters do. Their practices can provide many good ideas that you can borrow and use at your next inservice.

Theme it! If you plan a three-to-five-day professional growth experience for faculty, consider giving it a theme. This theme can then provide inspiration for activities, setting, and creature comforts. I had the good fortune to work for a week with a school corporation on K–12 curriculum design. The committee that organized the event chose a garden theme and did an excellent job pulling this into the task of curricular change. They sent colorful invitations decorated with clip-art flowers. They transformed a nondescript high school study hall into a comfortable room that "spoke" the theme. Inspirational growth and garden quotes decorated the walls, plants and fountains were placed throughout the room, a garden trellis invited everyone into the area where snacks and professional resources were available, garden centerpieces graced the tables, the door prizes were donated by a local nursery, and each day began with an activity centering around growing and nurturing the curricular changes they were creating. The participants anticipated each day because they knew something creative and fun would be awaiting them upon their arrival. Much was accomplished during the week, and I attribute a great portion of the success to the wonderful job the committee did tying everything to the chosen theme.

Always leave them feeling good and wanting more. It is important to have some thoughtful way of concluding your workshop or retreat. It can be as simple as a positive summary statement by you, the organizer, or as elaborate as a celebratory meal with presentations. Drawing closure to your event in an upbeat, motivating way leaves people feeling good about themselves and the workshop. Help them synthesize what they have accomplished and learned. This enables them to see the value in the time they invested. Provide an opportunity for them to give thought to how they will use and apply the information to their classroom practices.

At the end of the week-long curriculum workshop I mentioned earlier, the organizers planned a lovely catered luncheon for everyone. At the conclusion of the meal, a school board member presented everyone with a certificate of participation beneath the garden trellis. This certificate was printed on botanical stationary and was accompanied by a laminated bookmark covered with pressed flowers. All inexpensive ideas, but very meaningful to the teachers who received them. The school board member making the presentation also gave value and importance to the job they had done throughout the week.

Another easy treat to provide your group is dismissing them a few minutes early. People resent being kept longer than the designated ending time. Many have scheduled other events and delaying their departure creates feelings of negativity. Letting them go even ten minutes early is always a morale booster and helps them leave feeling there is time to spare in getting to their next meeting or scheduled appointment. They leave the workshop feeling upbeat and better in control of their time.

Giving people a small token at the end as a remembrance can also create good feelings about the workshop or retreat. These can be as elaborate or simple as your budget allows. For important, lengthy events, you might consider a specially designed T-shirt or plaque to commemorate the occasion. But for a half-day or daylong workshop, simply standing at the door and thanking everyone for coming will suffice. A special pencil or pen, a new mug, or a book that complements the workshop content are additional ideas for tokens of appreciation. As the school leader, you might also consider a follow-up thank-you note to teachers for their participation. This personal touch can mean a great deal.

ADDITIONAL RENEWAL OPPORTUNITIES

Study groups. Many school leaders create study groups for teachers with similar interests and goals. These groups meet regularly to discuss successful teaching approaches, current articles, related books, workshops attended, and so forth. Anything that applies to their area of interest is free for discussion during this time. These teachers become support for one another and encourage peer collaboration. School leaders are encouraged to participate in these groups on a regular basis. Your presence shows the teachers you value their participation and (who knows!?) you might even learn something!

Another type of study group can take the role of literature study or literature circles. The school leader provides teachers with an article or book that will be discussed at literature discussion time. Participants are asked to have read the article or a certain number of chapters in the book by the time the group meets. When the study group gathers together, they spend time reflecting, questioning, sharing, analyzing, and synthesizing the content of the book or article. These study groups can meet before or after school, at the school building, or at a site away from the school. This provides an opportunity for professional thought and sharing. In education, we don't often take the time to reflect upon what we read. We encourage our students to do this, but don't practice it ourselves. Literature study groups allow teachers to discuss professional literature and learn from others' perceptions and analyses.

Field trips. Visiting other schools and places of learning offers a fun way to get out of your familiar school environment and see what exciting things are happening elsewhere. A vanload of teachers visiting another building can leave the experience with fresh ideas, new perspectives, and sometimes a new appreciation for their own work environment. The field trip destination can be as simple as a school across town or as elaborate as a school in another state or country.

Social gatherings. Social gatherings, just for fun, are also opportunities for faculty and staff to cultivate personal renewal. A fall hayride, a winter soup supper, a spring progressive dinner, or a summer swimming party are all fun and carefree ways to gather staff together in an enjoyable way. Sharing time with our colleagues away from the school routine encourages camaraderie and provides the chance to see our coworkers as people beyond their teaching roles.

Many schools have a social committee designed for the purpose of organizing these types of gatherings. This group can take suggestions from the faculty and plan a calendar of events for the school year. These opportunities to be together in relaxed, social settings are important as a staff learns about each other and works to feel comfortable with their peers.

THE IMPORTANCE OF IT ALL

As a school leader, you must consider and plan carefully all of the renewal opportunities for faculty. Give attention to detail and look for ways to make the event special. Most importantly, make the staff feel supported and cared for during these events. Your extra effort can make the difference in whether the workshop or retreat is a success or failure. These events directly affect morale and thus, the effect on classroom practice can truly bring a sense of renewal to the whole organization.

PART 5

SPECIAL IS AS SPECIAL DOES

13

BUILDING AND ENHANCING YOUR MORALE

As educational leaders, we spend a tremendous amount of time and energy taking care of others. This may include solving problems, listening when others are upset, or working to increase the morale of those we work with. We wrote this book knowing that the ability to accomplish these tasks is an essential part of being an educational leader. However, this chapter we devote to the most important person in your school—**you!**

THINKING SELFISHLY

The idea of thinking selfishly may seem offensive to educators. After all, we are in a giving profession. However, if thinking selfishly can assist you in being able to be more effective in giving to others, would you consider it? It is critical that we focus on ourselves in order to be the positive and productive leaders that we need and want to be. Let's look at how our frame of mind can affect many others.

If, as principal, I am less than patient with a teacher, their frame of mind could easily be diminished. If that teacher then goes into the classroom and has a more negative approach to the students, then it is more likely that some incident will occur during that class that may result in an office referral. And, if I am also the principal who handles discipline, then I will be the one who now deals with this problem. Thus, my disposition will be negatively affected. Again, if I do not have a way to make sure that my approach toward others is positive, then my interactions are likely to be even more negative with students and teachers, which will create even more problems that I have to deal with.

This example may be simplistic, but I have tremendous confidence that over time, this scenario is played out on a daily basis in schools. The opposite is also true. If someone compliments me, then I am more likely to pass along that compliment to someone else. If we can boost others' frame of mind, then they can do the same. It becomes a self-fulfilling prophecy.

The situation recalls the old saying, "If a child feels stupid, he will act stupid, but if a child feels special, he will act special." It is just like being on a diet. Compliment me on my appearance and I won't even eat that last cookie!

IF YOU CAN'T TAKE CARE OF YOU . . .

Taking care of those around us and especially those we work with is a consistent challenge for any educational leader. However, in order to be able to sustain these efforts, which a leader must, it is essential that we in leadership roles first take care of ourselves. Because if we do not take care of ourselves, then we will be unable to take care of anyone else either.

How can those who are in the demanding role of a principal, superintendent, department chair, or team leader focus on themselves? When is there time? Is there any way to do it at work? Answering these questions is a critical link to being an effective morale enhancer in our school.

As educational leaders we *must* make sure we have a positive outlook each day. And if we are not feeling very positive about ourselves then it is difficult, if not impossible, to maintain this outlook. If we have a chip on our shoulder, then we do not want to be cheered up. Yet it is essential for the leader to maintain a persona that sets the tone for the organization. Whether they mean to or not, the building leaders establish the tone for the entire school. When the principal sneezes, the entire school catches a cold.

The leader must be able to have outlets away from work that allow for this personal rejuvenation. These things can include exercise (one of my keys is focusing on how you feel when you are done, not how you feel while you are doing it!), attending professional conferences, spending time with family or friends, or even watching a certain movie or reading a book that you know puts you in a positive frame of mind. One of my favorites is the black-and-white holiday classic "It's A Wonderful Life!" When I feel most down or sorry for myself, if I can make myself sit down for two hours and watch "It's A Wonderful Life!" I am rejuvenated for weeks. But the real challenge is, when I least feel like it, making myself do it.

In addition to things we can do outside of the work day, it is critical that all educators have things they can do while at work that allow them to reestablish a positive attitude and focus. We are going to focus on four things that any educational leader can do at work so that any time they want they can have a more positive outlook on school and life.

So, This Is Why We Have School

One of the challenges that all principals face is the number of problems that regularly come their way. They get to deal with kids when they are in trouble, parents when they are upset, and teachers when they have a problem. No matter how positive an outlook on life someone has, there is no question that this can be draining. When this occurs, the principal has to be self-aware enough to realize what is occurring and do something to remind themselves why they became a principal.

An approach that is a favorite of ours is very simple. When you are feeling overwhelmed, go into some classrooms. Even if you can only do so for 10 minutes, make it a point to visit several teachers' classes. It can remind you what school is all about. And, when you are the most down, go into your superstars' classes. It is amazing, but even three minutes in your best teacher's classroom can provide a quick reminder of why you became an educator.

If you are feeling so sorry for yourself that even visiting your best teacher's class does not work, there is one more room you can visit. When you most feel that life dealt you a rough hand, take five minutes and visit your multiple-handicapped classroom. I always felt that if I ever visited the multiple-handicapped classroom in my school and left feeling sorry for myself, then I was really in trouble. It is astonishing, but it never fails to help put things in perspective.

In addition to visiting classrooms when you need a boost, use the strategy as preventive medicine. If you can set aside a few minutes each day to go in classes and observe kids, teachers, and instruction, it can help you approach your job in a more positive light every day.

Obviously, one of the challenges in visiting classrooms is having time to do it. Many principals have a system worked out that allows them to visit classes daily. However, I found that if I just hoped to get into classrooms that day, I never did. Instead, I learned to pull out my personal calendar each Monday morning and write in times to visit classes each day. This process is described more thoroughly in Chapter 8.

In other words, I would find five to thirty minutes on Monday, Tuesday, Wednesday, etc. to go into classes. I would also designate the grade level or part of the building I was going to visit. This allowed me to avoid going into the same few classrooms at the same time. So, on Monday I would visit the seventh grade wing from 1:15 to 1:30. Tuesday, it would be the sixth grade classes from 9:10 to 9:20, Wednesday, exploratory classes from . . . and so on.

Scheduling this in my personal calendar forced me to set aside a few minutes for regular classroom visits. Keeping it private protected me during those inevitable times when something came up that I *had* to do, so I could not go into classes that day. When I was fortunate enough to add an assistant principal, we would touch base on Monday morning and do this process together. We each would visit different classes, but we both made it a point to regularly observe instruction. This may be even more necessary for the mindset of an assistant principal than it is for the principal! But it is an important part of taking care of yourself, so that you are more capable of taking care of others.

AS LONG AS YOU ARE IN THERE

To reemphasize a point made earlier in the book, these opportunities when you are in classrooms can take on an additional function. We mentioned earlier that when you visit a series of classes you can take along a notepad. When you are in the last classroom, you can write a note to any of the staff members that you visited regarding something positive you observed or heard. It can be anything from their approach to instruction to a new bulletin board (remember, we can never be praised too much!). Well, obviously this is morale-building for our staff members. Recall though that every time we praise, at least two people feel better—and one of them is *you.*

So that same activity that can boost someone else's morale can also boost yours. It is amazing, but if as an educational leader I have complimented a teacher numerous times, they actually listen when I make a suggestion. Additionally, if you can continually acknowledge the efforts of others, their willingness to go the extra mile for you and more importantly, for their students, increases dramatically.

PRAISE FOR STUDENTS AND PARENTS CAN BE FOR YOU, TOO

As a principal, the more I contact parents and say positive things about their child, the easier my job becomes. My relationships with students and families are strengthened, their acceptance of future not-so-good news is enhanced, and their perception of our school improves. Again, maybe the most important aspect of approaching students and parents in this positive light is that it makes me feel better. Additionally, it is much easier to maintain a productive frame of mind if others treat me with greater respect, but regardless, every time we seek out these positive contacts we have a more appropriate and productive outlook on work and life.

ATTABOY! (AND GIRL!)

In addition to all of the benefits we receive by recognizing the work of others, we still need an easy-access support system of our own. If we are at home, maybe we can go out for a jog. But if we are in our office or classroom at work, we still need a quick fix. Well, something that every educational leader—no, make that every educator—needs is an attaboy or attagirl file. We need a place where we keep positive notes we have received from our supervisors, peers, parents, or students. We can also include articles in the paper about our school, inspirational sayings or quotes, or other mementos that remind us how important we are and how critical our role as an educator is.

We may have a desk drawer where we tuck these things away. We may literally have a file where we keep these reminders. It is essential that *every* teacher, principal, and support staff member collect these gems. Interestingly, informal queries to educators across the United States indicate that about one-third of the teachers and principals accumulate these things for ready reference. The small number is a shame, because teachers have more opportunity to develop an attaboy file than any other profession. Each day we have student work that we might include. Teachers often receive notes, cards, and so forth acknowledging their efforts. As educational leaders we can be a great resource in providing notes of recognition and praise that others can save and cherish. The real challenge, though, is not developing an attaboy or attagirl file. The real challenge is—when we least feel like it, when we most feel sorry for ourselves, when we are at the bottom of our self-worth reservoir—taking our file out and reading it. And, as educators, we have to do this.

We cannot afford to approach our work, and more importantly, we cannot afford to have contact with students, without a positive outlook. It is critical that all educators approach each day in a positive frame of mind. We have to take care of ourselves because we have chosen a profession when each day we are taking care of so many others. You are worth it.

14

MAKING EVERYBODY FEEL LIKE SOMEBODY

A critical part of the job of an educational leader is to make sure that everyone in our organization feels special. Being aware of this on a daily basis is an important part of building staff morale. This is true whether we are a building-level leader, a department chair, or a team leader in a middle school. Examining how everyone feels and being sensitive to what is important to them is a critical component of enhancing the morale of everyone in our organization. One important part of this is showing interest and concern for all of our staff members' personal lives. This is not to be intrusive, but to demonstrate a high regard for their personal concern and wellbeing.

In addition to encouraging knowledge of our staff beyond school, this chapter provides many other ideas that can help an educational leader make everybody feel like somebody. After all, we are modeling what we expect all staff members to do with the students they work with each day.

TAKING CARE OF TEACHERS

In 1989, Adams and Bailey discussed the importance of principals taking care of their teachers. This care involved supporting teacher preferences, promoting feelings of self-efficacy, and focusing on the wellbeing of teachers through enhanced working conditions. The way teachers feel about themselves is a direct result of the leadership patterns and styles of principals. Through their leadership, principals should provide a belief in people, job and role diversity, high expectations, positive reinforcement, and celebrations of good performance. Teachers who feel good about themselves will become inspired to teach and deliver instruction at an exceptionally high level. Principals who take the time necessary to make sure that teachers understand their worth will find that classroom instruction will improve as teachers' self-efficacy improves.

To further demonstrate the power of teacher self-worth, Purkey (1983) found that research lends evidence that when teachers understand, accept, and like themselves, they have a much greater capacity to understand, accept, and like their students. Further research indicates that principals who demonstrate positive self-worth will act positively. They show a high regard for their employees as human beings and make continuous attempts to build the self-esteem of their staff members (Beck and Hillmar 1987).

There are many ways that a principal can take care of teachers, ways that help promote a positive environment in a school. Being aware of the personal side of teachers, showing interest in their families and children, and having a sensitivity to their outside interests are very valuable tools. When a teacher has been absent from school because of a child's illness or their own, the principal who makes it a point to seek out that teacher on their return to school and ask how they or their child feels will make headway toward helping teachers feel that they are valued.

KNOWLEDGE OF STAFF BEYOND SCHOOL

Just as the students who walk through our school doors each day are humans with lives beyond school, we must remember that our faculty and staff fall into this same category. They face family and civic obligations daily. As the leader of the school, the principal must be sensitive to these issues and help staff members bridge the gap between personal and professional worlds.

As the research showed, principals and teachers saw this as important part of a positive climate. Teachers were appreciative of these personal gestures of care and concern. This appreciation can affect the morale and disposition of faculty and staff. The ideas that follow have been shared by teachers and principals who found that an understanding of everyone's demands and lives beyond school is necessary. Appreciating the complex world that our staff members navigate can lead to productive relationships and a positive morale.

How Ya Doin'?

Day in and day out, conversation is a crucial part of building relations with your staff. This is a very simple concept, but one that takes sincere dedication and some of your valuable time. Face-to-face communication with a genuine sharing of thoughts and feelings is time well spent for a principal. Asking teachers about themselves, their family, and their lives helps that teacher know you care. You must sincerely listen and use this knowledge to help staff members through troubled times or difficult situations. This is also a time to let them share exciting news related to their lives. As the leader, you must learn to gently heal in times of strife and be one of the biggest cheerleaders in times of celebration. To do this, you must have knowledge. Day-in-and-day-out conversation is critical.

Sharp Tie You're Wearing Today!

We all appreciate it when our daily efforts to look presentable are noticed. Most professionals work hard on their appearance and enjoy when it is recognized. Taking the time to compliment a new addition to a staff member's wardrobe or a stylish haircut can mean a lot to people. They appreciate the acknowledgement of their efforts and this can boost self-esteem. It also provides motivation to continue to look your best because it feels good to be complimented.

What a Cutie!

A fun way for all to remember everyone's humble beginnings is to create a bulletin board of baby pictures of every staff member. Have each staff member bring in a baby picture and create an attractive display of these adorable pictures. You can number each photo and provide a key on the bulletin board or just put their names under the photos. You could also create a contest with the numbered photos by offering a prize to the first person who can turn in the correct teacher's name with the corresponding baby picture number. This is a fun "Back to School" bulletin board that will have everyone guessing, smiling, sharing, and laughing.

FACULTY SCAVENGER HUNT

Gather together one interesting fact about each of your faculty members. Your secretary can assist in this by asking each teacher to submit one thing about themselves that they think no one knows or just a few know. Compile all of these on a sheet of paper in statements like "find your coworker who climbed a mountain this summer" or "find your coworker whose first car was a brown Chevy Vega." Leave a blank next to each phrase and turn your faculty loose with this at a meeting or retreat. This is a fun way to learn more about each other and bring our everyday life into the school setting. This activity is guaranteed to be filled with laughter and fun.

TEACHER OF THE WEEK

Many teachers invite each student to become the student of the week. That student has a whole bulletin board to decorate and fill with items depicting their families, hobbies, interests, travels, and so on. Why not try this same concept with your faculty and staff? Designate a bulletin board or display case that can be used for this purpose. Set up a calendar assigning one week for each staff member to become the featured "teacher of the week." That teacher puts together a display about themselves that will help both teachers and students get to know more about them. Make sure you include secretaries, custodians, nurses, and cooks. This can inspire great creativity and it's almost guaranteed everyone will learn something new that they didn't know about each staff member. You might couple this with the Friday Focus Featured Folks idea presented in Chapter 6.

INFO AT YOUR FINGERTIPS

This tip is for those of us who have great difficulty remembering names and dates. When your social committee gathers personal data (names of family members, birthday, anniversary, favorite color) for its files or for secret pal exchanges, ask to have copies for your office. Keep these close at hand for the times you just can't seem to remember the name of your second grade teacher's middle daughter. This information could save you embarrassment and provide useful facts about the teachers you are trying to connect with.

SEND IT THROUGH THE MAIL

Many educational leaders are excellent about writing notes of praise and encouragement to teachers. If you are one of these people, I applaud you. Placed in teachers' mailboxes, these notes boost morale and spirit during the school day. Give thought to periodically sending notes to the teacher's home through the U.S. mail, especially cards or notes that deal with personal issues that the teacher is facing. Teachers appreciate the time it took for you to do this and it is a gentle reminder to them of your awareness that life goes on beyond the school day.

In addition, a quick phone call at home can also be greatly appreciated by your staff. This is especially appropriate when you have teachers going through a difficult situation that you are sure they don't want to talk about at school. The two of you can converse through the privacy of the telephone, and you can make sure that they know you care and are thinking of them. You can also ask if there are any errands you could run for them or meals you could arrange for. Many times they will not need your services, but the caring phone call can mean so very much.

SHARING IN JOY AND IN SORROW

Attending your staff's family functions, when appropriate, can mean more than you will ever know. I recall a principal telling about attending the marriage of her new first grade teacher. The wedding was a five-hour drive away in a different state, but she made sure she was there. She told me that the teacher was so moved when she saw her come through the receiving line that she began to cry. This principal also received a personal note from the bride's parents thanking her for making the long journey. They were greatly impressed with the personal thoughtfulness the principal showed and shared that they were so thankful their daughter was fortunate enough to work for her.

Sometimes these events aren't easy ones. Distance can make it difficult and the occasion isn't always a joyous wedding. Funerals, memorial services, and visitations are time to show your concern for staff by your presence. Sometimes just a hug and words of sympathy are all that are needed. Your attendance shows them that you care and want to support them as they grieve an important loss. These gestures in times of celebration and suffering mean a great deal to people. Your personal concern and presence can mean so much.

THE BEST WAY TO A TEACHER'S HEART . . .

Don't forget the power of food. As the leader, you can provide food in fun and unexpected ways to let your staff know you care. After open house night, when your staff has put in a long and important evening, bring doughnuts or muffins the next morning. Arrange them on an attractive tray and place them in the lounge with a sign that says, "Thanks for a dynamite open house. You are the best!" Unexpected treats always bring a smile and are remembered.

We all know that food at faculty meetings is a must. Try to add some variety to this by tying in seasonal or holiday themes. See if your cafeteria might bake pumpkin-shaped cookies at Halloween or red and green cupcakes at Christmas. Try candy corn (fat free!) in the fall, candy hearts for Valentine's Day, or pastel M & Ms as Easter approaches. Jell-O Jigglers can bring a smile and lollipops will make your staff feel like kids again! A brightly colored serving bowl filled with a mixture of popcorn and pretzels is a healthy alternative to sweets. A crisp red apple at each seat is also a different twist to traditional fare. Be creative and share fun food ideas with other principals at district and regional meetings.

One principal makes sure that at the beginning of each month a birthday cake is placed in the lounge for all of those turning a year older during that month. There is a mini-celebration before school and he leads everyone in the singing of Happy Birthday to all the staff members affected. He then passes out his "birthday treat" to the celebrants. His gift is a certificate for a 30-minute release from their classes or duties, and he provides the coverage. This was described in Chapter 7 as "the ultimate birthday treat!"

A LITTLE CAN MEAN A LOT

Most of us have the traditional social gatherings in our schools at the beginning of the year, at the holiday season, and celebrating the end of a successful school year. These are always fun and a wonderful time to include spouses and families. Sometimes a missing piece to this school socialization is time for the staff to be out together and enjoy each other's company away from the school setting. You, as the leader, can coordinate small social outings that don't take a lot of planning or time. They can also be spontaneous, which adds some excitement to the event. Perhaps, after all the students are gone, you make an announcement over the intercom inviting all interested to join you for coffee at the new bookstore, ice cream at the local Dairy Queen, or even a game of putt-putt golf! Many staffs enjoy Happy Hour at a local pub on Fridays. Try to find a place that serves food, isn't smoky, and has nonalcoholic beverages for those who choose not to drink. You want to allow everyone to feel comfortable joining the fun.

Some principals and teachers organize Book Clubs that meet monthly for "Coffee and Conversation" regarding a specific title they have chosen to discuss. The books can be professional, but certainly don't have to be. These book discussions can be held in the mornings before school at a local diner that serves great breakfasts, after school at the malt shop, or in the evenings at a restaurant with a relaxing atmosphere. Of course, you could always meet at school, but sometimes it is nice to gather together away from the work environment.

Another avenue for socialization is through exercise. Organize a walking or running group within the school. Meeting times can vary and all who are interested can join in a healthy activity that promotes interaction between staff members. Sometimes the local YMCA or YWCA will offer exercise classes in your building, if you can get enough staff members to participate.

Perhaps you have a very musical staff. If so, organize a small band or chorus. For people who have interest in music, participating in casual musical activities can provide relaxation and enjoyment. Practice once a week and perform for the students at the end of the year. They will love it! You may soon be invited to perform for other school events—opening sessions, sporting events, banquets, and so on. Remember that you can always say no and keep the group "just for fun."

Look for small but effective ways to interact with staff members outside the school setting. Everyone leads busy and hectic lives in this day and age. Often 30 minutes spent over a cup of coffee with your coworkers can fit into your schedule more easily than a whole evening out. Search for creative ways to be with your staff members in relaxed, enjoyable activities that don't take up too much of everyone's precious time.

Christmas Cards with a Twist

One of the most memorable ways you can show your staff you really care is something that can be done at one of the most exciting times of the year—Christmas. Have someone (yourself, secretary, custodian, etc.) go to each classroom and take a picture of the teacher instructing and working with students. It is also fun and meaningful to include cooks, custodians, secretaries, bus drivers, nurses, and so on in this holiday treat. If they question why you are there, just tell them it is for the yearbook, a scrapbook, or a school display. Then ask your secretary to gather the addresses of your teachers' parents. This can be done through spouses (who need to be asked to keep this a secret), or the secretary can just ask for the information, telling the teachers you need it for personal files or emergency procedures. Most will comply, but others will be suspicious. If they persist in knowing why, just smile and tell them it is a Christmas secret!

Have Christmas cards made that are from the school. Many companies offer these at holiday time; regular cards from the store will work, too. Address each card with the name of the staff members' parents and insert the picture of their son or daughter doing their important job in the school. Take the time to write a short note to the parents, letting them know what a valued staff member their son or daughter is and how proud you are to be able to work with them each day. Seal them, stamp them, mail them, and smile. You will have touched many lives in a very unique and special way. This is an excerpt from a letter received by a principal who took the time to send these special cards.

> "You will never fully know the happiness you brought to us with your kind card. Tears came to our eyes as we read the dear words you wrote about our daughter. We have never before received such a letter. It means so much to us.
>
> "We are sure that our other five daughters are appreciated by those they serve, but we have never received a letter like yours. We shall never forget your kind words."

The little extra time and effort this gesture takes reaps benefits far beyond your knowledge and imagination. Good deeds harvest great rewards.

Your teachers must know that you possess personal concern and regard for them as individuals. Any of the ideas presented here can help you bridge the gap between the professional and the personal sides of your working relationship. Also remember that showing this interest and genuine caring for your staff is powerful modeling of how you want them to treat the children in their classrooms. The way you interact with and treat faculty and staff will set a tone of compassion and understanding in your school. This will eventually find its way to the students in school. And isn't that what it's all about?

15

NEW IS NOT JUST DIFFERENT, IT SHOULD BE BETTER!

One of the most effective ways to improve the morale of an organization is to hire people with better morale. Though this sounds simple, it is very much true. Remember, as we discussed earlier:

When we hire new staff members, we usually want our organization to become more like our new teachers than we want our new teachers to become like our organization.

In other words, we are continually hoping to hire people better than the average people in our organization. We are hoping for superstars with each hire, but at the very least, we are insistent on improving the talent in our group. One of our challenges, then, is to have these people, who are often "rate busters" when they are first hired, maintain that effort and enthusiasm level for as long as they are in our organization. In addition, our next goal is to have people move up and join them. We want these new people to exceed our "group norm" and eventually draw enough people up to their level that their new standard becomes the new group norm (Figure 6). In order to accomplish this, we have three areas of focus: selecting dynamite staff members, inducting them effectively into the organization, and then cultivating their leadership skills.

FIGURE 6

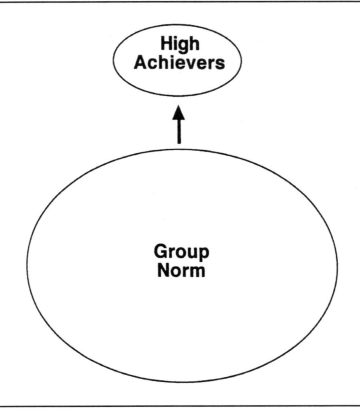

New positions that open in a school may be the most precious commodity there is. The approach a leader takes in selecting the teachers to fill the openings and the orientation provided to new staff members will determine to a large degree the future direction of the organization. Though sometimes the hiring process is all that is considered when employing new faculty members, the education (both formal and informal) they experience after becoming part of the staff is equally important. There are two basic ways to improve an organization: You can improve the people you have, or hire better people. The same is true with improving the morale in an organization: You can improve the morale of the people in your organization, or hire people with better morale. The vast majority of this book is dedicated to improving the morale of your existing staff. However, this chapter is devoted to employing individuals with positive morale and then, as their leader, helping them to maintain that morale.

HIRING NEW FACULTY

One of the most important determinants of any new position is the type of educator we need for our organization. Traditionally these have been broken down departmentally or by grade level. We commonly think, "Our position is in seventh grade science, so we need a seventh grade science teacher." This is true if a building leader is looking to simply "fill a position." However, if administrators are truly looking to develop an outstanding school, then they need to focus on consistently hiring great teachers. If the goal and expectations are to aim for hiring superstars, then even if we just get close, our school is likely to grow in the desired direction.

Unfortunately, like most things of value, the process of employing outstanding faculty members takes a great deal of work. If we engage in this process with the expectation of hiring a great teacher, then that can help us be successful in the employment process.

It is important to maintain a conscious effort to recruit quality candidates. When educators are at professional conferences or meetings, oftentimes other leading educators are there. Building relationships with teachers in other schools and areas can provide potential future employee candidates or people who may know of strong candidates. Making and establishing regular contact with university supervisors of student teachers is another method that can prove fruitful. Contact them as soon as the possibility of an opening occurs; ask if they have any outstanding teacher candidates this year or in the recent past. Inquiring whether any of these potential employees are among the best student teachers they have ever had the opportunity to work with is a way to determine if these potential teachers can meet your expectations.

When a leader is checking references and making calls to the previous (or sometimes current) employer, asking questions such as, Was (or is) this person the best teacher in your school?

or What are her/his leadership abilities? can help identify high-quality teachers. It may often happen that a more accurate description of the employee's ability will come from a previous employer, rather than a current one, because they probably do not have as much of a vested interest in that person's career.

Though many principals hope to hire teachers with experience when they have an opening in their school, we often felt that adding first-year teachers may be of more benefit. We were never opposed to adding veteran staff members, but it may be easier to establish and cultivate a higher standard in a school by adding new teachers.

New teachers are often chomping at the bit to make a difference. They have never "griped" in any teachers' lounge, and have no expectation of "following the language of the teacher contract." With staff members who are new to the profession, you may have more of a chance to cultivate them in your image than you have with experienced teachers. Sometimes leaders hesitate to employ first-year teachers because of potential "growing pains" or because of the need to provide more support in helping establish classroom management, but if you do a good job in the selection process, these people are often very willing to be molded into setting a new dynamic in the school.

Additionally, it may be easier to pair inexperienced teachers with your superstars, which can foster development of the peer group you hope to grow. Brand new teachers often are looking for a role model to emulate; creating this link is one of the opportunities to help establish a higher group norm in an organization. The other challenge for the educational leader is to help maintain these high expectations for the new staff members and to help these new staff members influence others. Keeping their morale at the original high level of excitement is a critical part of the leader's role. Enhancing their abilities to influence previous staff members is also very important.

When hiring staff, principals should always look at the leadership ability of the candidates and the way their personalities will fit into the rest of the school team. Knowing how this person will informally interact with the other faculty members can be an important element in the qualities they can provide a school. Involving other teachers, especially if the new staff will be on a team, can also help ensure the effectiveness of the relationships in the working environment.

If organizational leaders consistently pursue the standard of great teachers, they are much more likely to be able to raise the talent level and abilities of the teachers in their schools. Since the standard of greatness is the minimum we can have for the educational settings of our youth, each piece that is a part of the whole must be at that level also. Inducting new staff members and cultivating their ability to become positive school leaders go hand in hand and are an important responsibility of the effective educational leader.

NEW STAFF INDUCTION AND ORIENTATION

Duke (1989) found that acquiring a competent teaching staff is integral to a school's instructional effectiveness. The principal must play a key role in recruitment, inservice education, and staff motivation. Capable, skilled, and energetic teachers must be selected and made aware that their talents will be appreciated. After a robust faculty has been hired, it must be maintained and nurtured with ongoing staff development designed by teachers. The staff must be treated as professionals and encouraged to take leadership positions. If a school does not have proficient teachers, its instructional effectiveness is doomed.

Staff openings are very precious and it is essential that they be treated as such. Making sure that new faculty understand the role they need to play in the school if its effectiveness is to continue growing is very important in the hiring process. Sharing with interviewees that there is no pecking order in the school, that their opinions are as valuable as those of any other staff member, and that they are expected to focus continually on what is best for students can help establish and refine an appropriate environment in a school.

When adding new faculty, the principal should take care that the rookie teacher is exposed to positive forces. The new staff member's classroom should be located next to a teacher who will provide productive influence, and the conference period shared with staff members who can help shape an appropriate belief system. During the interview and hiring process, the principal should make clear which teachers on the staff the new faculty members should look to for guidance. The principal should also explain the need for new staff members to assume needed leadership roles in the school. It is important to establish this expectation early on.

When hiring a new staff member, the principal must establish guidelines and expectations for new staff. Statements like these can be an important first step:

"I do not believe in pecking orders in our school. I believe that all staff members are of equal importance. When I hire new staff, I want them to take a vocal leadership role in the school. I expect them to speak up at faculty meetings. Within the department (or grade level or team) it is essential that *all* staff, especially our new members, voice their opinions. If I did not want you to assume a leadership role in the school, I would not have hired you! You have wonderful ideas and are tremendously talented. I need and expect you to take a very visible role at staff meetings and other times when you feel you have something to contribute. I hired you because I want our school to benefit on a school-wide basis because of your talents and knowledge."

Having a dialogue like this in your first contact with a new staff member can be very empowering. It can give them the confidence to express their opinions and can help their influence infiltrate the school beyond their classrooms.

It is important that new faculty feel included as early as possible; using available time prior to the start of school is a valuable opportunity. A good first step is to have the new staff contact teachers to meet with them, or have positive teachers contact the newcomers. The principals should meet with the teachers, find out what supplies they might need, and support them by providing as many as possible. Taking them out to lunch and providing them with a staff T-shirt, business cards, and a school mouse pad are examples of ways to help the teachers quickly feel that they are a part of the school and staff. This informal time can also provide additional opportunities to visit about curriculum and about the philosophies and management styles of both the principal and the newcomer.

It is always exciting to take new staff members out to lunch at a nice local restaurant. Imagine the look on their faces as you approach the table to find a staff T-shirt neatly folded on their plate, and business cards with our school logo and their name professionally printed. Talk about a positive start to their school year! And your secretary will love to sneak out to the restaurant early to make these arrangements. What a way to give the morale of new staff a boost and take another step towards building tremendous loyalty between you and the new staff member.

Organizational leaders should provide a high level of new faculty development for all rookie staff members. Whether or not they have teaching experience, they should become familiar with the expectations of appropriateness in the school where they are now working. Having weekly meetings for the first six to nine weeks of school would be one way to build collegiality among new staff, and also allow the principal of the school to cultivate relations with the freshman faculty as well as expose them to the staff leaders they would like them to model.

Our school held eight meetings at the start of the year for new faculty, at 7:15 A.M. every other Tuesday. The sessions covered a variety of topics, ranging from classroom management to the role of the counselor. Spreading the sessions over the beginning of the year gave the new teachers a more manageable experience than compressing all of the information into two or three days before the start of school. The other purpose, though, had little to do with content. It had to do with building relations between new staff and the most positive and productive staff members in the school.

In a session on classroom management, two of the most effective, positive teachers could lead the group. When discussing the counseling program, involve the most talented counselor. Let a particularly effective special education teacher work with new staff. The new faculty then have the chance to become oriented to the procedures of the school as well as the opportunity to build relations with the "right" staff members. This encourages the faculty to continue to grow in a positive way. If you have several new staff members in any year, this also allows them to become more cohesive and helps them to work together to maintain the higher "new" standard you hope they establish.

One of the sessions could center around inviting new staff

members to evaluate you. This idea, also discussed in Chapter 8, offers a wonderful way to give the newcomers a chance to interact with you regarding the evaluation process and to see you in the role of a teaching peer.

Another session could take place before the school year starts or at one of these early-morning meetings. You could load all of the new staff members in one vehicle (a school bus if needed!) and drive them around the community, especially the attendance area where your school's students reside. This will help give them a feel for the area and provide them with some perspective regarding the home situations of the students they will work with. If you wanted, you could invite other key staff members to be the tour guides or join you on the journey.

When the opportunity arises to add new staff, principals need to ensure that they hire outstanding candidates and then structure their initial contact with the school in a way that will allow them to build relations that will best influence the new staff and the entire school. Providing opportunities like these will allow for positive interactions between and among staff members.

CULTIVATING LEADERSHIP

Administrators should talk openly and honestly with new and existing faculty about leadership and the need for it. At first, this should be primarily in one-on-one or small-group discussions, but eventually it will be with the entire faculty. It is important that as new staff members join a faculty, they become part of the ever-growing influential direction. Eventually, the entire staff will move over to the positive side of the fence. This task, like most processes of growth and change within a school, cannot be accomplished without the leadership of the school's informal teacher leaders.

Successful principals are more able to identify the informal leaders in their schools and use them effectively to help lead their schools in a direction that benefits students. Adding new staff members with leadership skills and then cultivating those skills is an essential part of effectively selecting and inducting new staff. Shifting the focus from hiring a good teacher to adding a great teacher-leader changes the context in which educational leaders operate.

A team leader at a middle school can benefit immeasurably when a dynamic teacher joins the team. The environment across the entire fourth grade or throughout the high school English department can shift dramatically with the addition of one of two positive staff members. This same focus is true in employing any staff members. Whether you are a principal adding a teacher or the head custodian adding someone to the night shift, the personalities you choose can have a much broader effect than you may first realize. It is much easier to hire a great employee than it is to fire a mediocre one!

PART 6

FOCUSING OUTSIDE THE STAFF TO AFFECT STAFF MORALE

16

FEELING AT HOME WHILE AT WORK— ENHANCING THE PHYSICAL PLANT

Think about the number of hours you spend at work. I'm sure most of you spend seven to ten hours a day at your workplace—to say nothing of the nights and weekends you put in extra hours to finish projects and prepare for future events. If you are going to spend this much time in one place, then the place should be comfortable, inviting, and easy to work in. Creating this kind of environment is within your control. It doesn't entail spending a lot of money or even buying new furniture. You can take what you have and create a work atmosphere that invites you in and makes the daily tasks you must complete seem not so overwhelming.

I can't help but think of my own office. A renovated dorm room, it was built with efficiency in mind, not comfort. The concrete walls and metal shelving do not exude any warmth or comfort, but I was not to be denied an office that welcomed me each day! Some cheery curtains, a plush rug, cushions for the chairs, pictures on the walls, and some silk plants quickly made this a place I wanted to come into each day. I also do my very best to keep things shelved, put away, and filed. Now I must admit that at times my stacks get plentiful, but an occasional hour or so devoted to organizing and filing can make all the difference. When I enter my office and it is in order, I am much more productive. I am not depressed by the clutter and piles of "mystery" correspondence and handouts. I know what needs to be done and am not distracted by an office in disarray.

Let's translate all of this to the place we call school. Whitaker (1997) found that in schools with a more positive climate, the atmosphere was orderly, warm, and inviting. Most of you can probably picture these schools—the schools that just feel right when you walk in. Even before you talk to anyone, you know what the school stands for and you can tell it is student-centered. As a school leader, this should be your goal. You want people get a strong sense of the personality of your school as they walk up the front steps and enter the doors. Once inside, the climate of the school should be visibly evident. The foyer should be welcoming, and so should the office area. The physical presence of the school should portray the climate and personality of the students and staff inside.

If you do not feel that you personally have an "eye for decorating," this is not a problem. Empower teachers, staff, parents, and even students with talents in this area; have them assume an active role in the transformation. I knew of a high school principal who was convinced that the physical appearance of a building was an essential part of establishing a positive and productive school climate. However, he admitted that he had no idea how to make anything look good. He put a secretary, a teacher, and a parent in charge and turned them loose. The result was remarkable and it even made him look good!

Before we move into the "ideas" section of this chapter, you might be asking how this ties into morale. One exercise I do with my pre-service teachers is called a "climate hunt." The building where we have class has fifteen floors. Each floor houses a different department, and each has an entrance foyer that people travel through to get to the offices. Some foyers are cheery and welcoming; others look institutional and barren. The students are instructed to travel to different floors, not speaking to anyone as they move from level to level. They are to take notes on how they feel and record their first impressions on the various floors. When they return to class, we discuss their findings. They speak of feeling "welcome, excited, inspired" on the floors with attractive entrances. In turn, they share their feelings of "despair, depression, sadness" when they visit the floors with little visual interest. We then discuss which floors we might like to work on and why. Naturally, they all choose to work on the floors that feel welcoming—where the "upbeat tone," "positive feel," and "purposeful design" make them feel comfortable. We discuss how our classrooms must be designed to create warm and inspiring climates for our students. Upbeat, positive, and purposeful are some of the exact words we would like to use when describing classroom atmosphere.

This simple activity helps us see the power of the look and feel of a building and how this can affect the attitude and morale of the people who work there. This activity can be used in any setting. A middle school team could examine their hallway; a high school department could reflect on the appearances of their part of the building.

You want your staff to be uplifted when they walk in, you want them to feel comfortable, and you want them to be inspired to do their very best work while in the school. Time spent on your physical environment is time well spent, not only for the staff, but for the students, for the community, and even for you.

GETTING YOUR STAFF TO BUY IN

When I became a principal, I was fortunate enough to become the administrator of a building that, overall, had a dedicated and bright staff. For the past four years, these teachers had worked hard on curriculum development and instructional pedagogy, building a very solid foundation. On the other hand, while I could tell that the physical environment was clean and orderly, it lacked that warm and inviting appeal you want a building to have. In one of my administrator preparation courses, we had visited a school that exuded a positive climate throughout the building. From the minute we walked in, our sense of comfort and invigoration was established. The day was spent observing, talking to teachers, interacting with students, and conversing with the principal. After seeing and "feeling" the school, we all left so motivated and inspired. I began to ponder

how I could make a school look and feel this way. My task began as a solo pursuit, but soon turned into a building-wide effort.

During the summer before I began my first year, I spent time
transforming the lounge and the outer office. I painted, stenciled, and organized bulletin boards. I was fortunate enough to
have springs sticking out of the lounge furniture, so that I could
plead for some new comfortable pieces for the staff. We stenciled in the office, added some prints I made out of old calendar
pictures and inexpensive frames, and popped a silk floral arrangement on the counter. A crafty parent with a hot-glue gun
decorated a large grapevine wreath with "school" items—pencils, markers, rulers, pens, a box of crayons, scissors—all topped
with a bow made of ribbon printed with bright red apples. We
hung this in front of the office as a welcome signal to all who
entered. I also added a wooden bench in front of the office and
placed flowers on a table beside it. We also spent time making
the faculty restroom a little less bland. A little paint, some shelving, pictures, attractive towels, a rug, and some material Velcro-
ed to the sink as a skirt to cover cleaning supplies added an
"executive" touch to a once drab and institutional restroom.

It was interesting to see how these changes began to have a
"domino" effect with the faculty and staff. The custodian and
secretary joined in the fun as they began to notice the uplifting
results. When the staff arrived, they too took notice, and before
I knew it they were volunteering their talents by sewing, painting, and stenciling. Once everyone was back and began to see
the transformations, there were informal conversations about
how these changes could be continued into other parts of the
school. I told the staff about the school I had visited, and we
decided to take vanloads of teachers on a trip there. Most of the
faculty were able to see the school, returning with many wonderful ideas. These ideas and many additional ones will be shared
in this chapter.

Remember that this transformation began with the school
leader setting the stage for change in a non-threatening way. No
one was asked to do anything. Starting as small projects in the
office and lounge, the improvements eventually spread throughout the entire school. Some staff will always be more enthusias-

tic than others, but that is fine. Just remember, any improvement is movement in the right direction and better than where you began. Also keep in mind that transforming a whole school takes time. Just take it project by project, and enjoy your small successes along the way.

I encourage you, as a first step, just to walk around the building, inside and out. Try to pretend you are moving to the area, and look through the critical eye of a potential new resident. What do you see? Is the school a place that invites you in? Is it orderly and well maintained? Is it warm and friendly? Is it a place you would want your own children to attend? If these questions are difficult to answer, then there is work to be done. But this work can be fun, because the rewards are so visually uplifting and motivating!

THE EXTERIOR OF THE SCHOOL

As you walk around the outside of the building, take note of overall maintenance. Check windows, paint, sidewalks, guttering. If you feel you are not qualified to make judgments on these, invite your custodian or maintenance director to walk around with you. Make a "wish list" of improvements to the outside of the school. See if you can get a few things done each year with the help of the district maintenance crew.

Take note of landscaping possibilities. Think about adding shrubs, bushes, trees, and flowers. A local nursery might help you with design options and possibly give you a discount on services. School clubs and organizations are often in search of service learning opportunities. Beautifying the outside of the school can become an excellent project for them. Your school parent organization is another option for money and physical help with this endeavor. Consider benches and waste receptacles. Placed attractively, these can enhance the outer look of the building and also be functional.

THE ENTRANCE DOORS AND FOYER

Make sure that your entrance is welcoming and well maintained. Keep doors painted and glass clean. Include a sign that welcomes visitors to your school and politely requests them to check in at the office. One principal told me he placed a sign on the door that read, "Please come to the office so we can warmly welcome you." He used this wording purposefully. He said, "If those words are there, then we have to be sure we are *doing* it!"

Once inside the doors, use the foyer to set the tone for the rest of the building. Display children's work, paint a mural, use plants, include attractive benches if possible. Many schools display their mission statements, professionally framed, so that all can see the true purpose of your school. One school even has a couple of rocking chairs in the foyer with a basket of books on a table between them. This adds a touch of comfort for mothers waiting with young children and serves as a wonderful reading area for volunteers working with students.

This area is an integral "first impression" spot. Many people will form their opinion of the school based on the feeling they have in the first few minutes after they enter the building. Continuously monitor this area so it is not neglected. Make sure it is clean, attractive, and welcoming. You can also have a PTA committee that is responsible for "entrance appearance." Empowering an interested group of parents can assure that students, staff, and visitors have a dynamic first impression each day. Assigning the appearance of different parts of the school to different groups is a way to "spread the wealth" and help school-wide pride infiltrate throughout the school. One middle school does this by advisory group, but rotates the areas—the foyer, the cafeteria, each hallway—each month, so that every student and staff member has some ownership of the entire building.

THE SCHOOL OFFICE

This is another area where first impressions are made. Probably one of the most crucial elements in the office is the smile and warm greeting of the school secretary or principal. This costs no money and can reap great rewards. I'll never forget the feeling I got the time I entered a school office and the secretary was on the phone with a friend, discussing last night's football game and how unruly the students were. She knew I was there, yet kept her conversation going, initiating even more banter about the students' behaviors. I tried not to listen, but it was impossible. I looked around the office for a place to sit. There were a couple of chairs shoved in a corner. The first chair I chose was unstable, so I looked at the other one, but it was so dirty, I didn't want to move. There were piles of dust in the corners on the floor and a couple of wilted plants on the counter. As I sat there, another staff member walked through the office, looked at me, frowned, and walked away. Finally the principal came out of his office and asked if he could help me. I told him I was there for an appointment with him and followed him into his private office, as the secretary's conversation droned on.

Needless to say, this first impression was quite negative. Even though the office appearance was neglected, the secretary's behavior was what really stuck in my mind. If she had only been professional enough to greet me, smile, and conclude her phone conversation, the neglected office wouldn't have seemed so pitiful.

The first words spoken to visitors and the manner in which they are spoken set a powerful tone for these important guests. Help the office staff and teachers understand this. Model appropriate behavior and compliment them when situations are handled in a pleasant and professional way. Remind them to be professional in all conversations that take place in the office, especially when students are present. Students' ears hear everything and they usually can't wait to get home or back to the classroom to share their overheard "news."

The office area should be attractive and orderly. Fresh paint, plants, and pictures take little time, yet can add so much to a significantly visible area of your school. An elementary school I recently spent some time in had a border of colorful handprints around the office. When I asked about it, the principal told me that every student in the school had his or her handprint somewhere in the building. Sure enough, I saw similar bright handprints in the cafeteria and hallways as well.

One high school I visited had added a simple wallpaper border around the office and professionally framed student artwork on the walls. Numerous cushioned chairs were available to sit in and educational magazines were set out on an attractive end table topped with a table lamp. The look was professional, clean, and comfortable. I was greeted by a warm smile and a secretary who made me feel at home immediately. These were simple additions to the office, but ones that set a positive tone and a welcoming message to visitors, community, staff, and students.

THE SCHOOL LEADER'S OFFICE

The office of the school leader sets an example and is an opportunity to model expectations. Keeping this work area clutter-free and attractive helps set a standard for the faculty and staff. Also allowing your personality to show itself in your office helps everyone see some of your tastes and interests. Many leaders keep pictures of family on their desks or on shelves in their offices. Personal collections can also add a nice touch. I knew of one principal who collected miniature tractor replicas and used them to adorn his shelving. An assistant middle school principal displayed his collection of bobbing-headed sports dolls. Framed diplomas and awards make a professional wall display. My favorite author/illustrator is Chris Van Allsburg. I always hang a framed enlargement of the cover of *The Polar Express* in my office. Greenery, rugs, and lamps for accent lighting can soften the edges of the traditional principal's office. Simple window treatments, purchased at a local discount store and hung with blinds, can help your office feel more comfortable. Many of these window treatments can be put on tension rods and slipped into the window casing without even having to attach rods to the walls.

Look carefully at your furniture arrangement. If possible, arrange your office so that your desk is not always between you and the person visiting your office. Some situations need not be formal, and it is beneficial to have an additional seating option in these instances. It is ideal to have an extra seating area where you can converse with someone without having your desk between the two of you. If space does not allow this, at least make sure there are two chairs on the other side of your desk so you can join your visitor there if you choose.

Another beneficial addition to your office, if space allows, is a table for small-group meetings and conferences with teachers. Again, this pulls interaction away from your formal desk area and participants feel more on an equal working level with you.

Many principals find this table a good place for pre- and post-observation conferences and grade-level or team meetings, as well as a great place to spread out special projects you are working on. I have also seen some principals hang dry-erase boards next to these tables to record meetings ideas or to keep track of goal attainment.

It is a good idea is to keep a basket of toys and books in your office for occasions when younger siblings accompany a visiting parent. These toys can help keep the child entertained so you and the parent can converse with minor interruption. Parents will appreciate your thoughtfulness, and you will value the quality meeting time with them.

THE STAFF LOUNGE

This is a place where everyone can enjoy the fruits of their labors and will appreciate the attention and interest in their comfort. Sprucing up the staff lounge is a great morale booster and can be as simple as creating usable, attractive bulletin boards. I went to a brand new school not too long ago where the staff lounge was filled with new furniture and a lovely kitchenette. This wonderful facility lacked warmth and interest. The bulletin boards were barren and the walls were drab. There was excellent shelving for what might have been a professional resource center, but I couldn't really tell what was on the shelves. It seemed to be a mishmash of books and magazines with no evident purpose. No one had given this area the attention it needed and deserved. Just some cheery bulletin-board greetings and an organized resource center would have added so much to this lounge for not a lot of time and effort.

I have seen lounges where the school leaders have taken the time to create a place where their staff members can relax, converse, and share a cup of morning coffee. These spaces are filled with comfortable furniture, flowers on the tables, bulletin boards with purpose, window treatments, rugs or carpeted areas, and inspirational pictures or posters on the walls. A comfortable and relaxing haven can give many teachers inspiration and the opportunity for renewal throughout the day. Some principals keep chalkboards or dry-erase boards in the lounges for quick staff updates or uplifting quotes. Bulletin boards can be organized into sections providing a variety of information. One section can be used to share flyers for upcoming workshops and conferences, one can be used for district information, another can post your weekly staff memo, the lunch menu, the school newsletter, and the like. Teachers will appreciate having this information for easy referral during breaks or lunchtime conversations. Some lounges also house professional resources (books, magazines, and videos). I know one principal who highlights one resource each week. He displays it on the top of the resource bookcase with a short written "book talk" sharing important and interesting aspects of the book. This keeps teachers aware of what's available and is a way to showcase new resources as they are added.

I often hear principals lament about negative talk in the staff lounge. We all know that your job does not allow you to be in the lounge all day monitoring staff discussions. But we do know that people in an upbeat, inspirational, and comfortable environment are less likely to be negative and cynical. Creating a lounge that is bright, cheerful and inviting is one positive step to thwarting less than productive conversations in your staff lounge.

HALLWAYS

Hallways are some of the most traveled areas in any school. Don't underestimate the power they have to create visual interest and learning opportunities. Many schools do an excellent job of filling their hallways with student work and visually attractive displays. Others neglect this area and treat them as only a practical area for student movement. Encourage teachers to display student work by adding bulletin boards or cork stripping down the hallway.

One of my fifth grade teachers used her area of the hallway to create a hall of presidents. Her students drew and researched each president. Their research report and drawings were displayed in chronological order in the hallway. Another time, the same teacher used her section of the hallway to re-create a visual representation of our Milky Way Solar System. With papier-mâché and paint, the students constructed scale models of the planets. These were hung from the ceiling, using the entire hallway to re-create in scale the order from the sun and the distance each planet is from the sun. Research on the planets and other space facts were posted on the walls. This area became a learning environment for every student in the school. The hallway was on the second floor, but we had classes from the first floor taking trips upstairs to view and learn from these educational and student-made displays.

Use every inch of space you can. Attractively arrange tables and chairs in unused areas. I did this with some district furniture no one wanted. I picked out some old oak tables and chairs and during the slower winter months, a couple of workers from the maintenance crew refinished them. I placed them in stairwells and at the end of hallways. Teachers began to utilize them for small-group work and meetings. Students could use the area to read with a partner or have a nice desk area to complete unfinished work. This furniture also added a warmth and coziness to the stark hallways. I have seen many schools add table lamps, books, plants, beanbag chairs, and even rocking chairs to these areas, enhancing their visual appeal.

One of the easiest, cheapest, and quickest ways to brighten your hallways is by adding colorful striping. With some chalk lines and a few gallons of paint, you can add zip to your hallways instantly. Choose a couple of coordinating colors and paint a stripe down the hallway, with another below it. Consider making one stripe wider than the other (perhaps the first stripe 10 inches wide and the second 6 inches wide). If you are really adventurous, you can add peaks and zigzags to your design. Some schools have opted for bright geometric shapes painted throughout the hallways. These can create great visual interest in the school.

When I approached my custodian with the striping idea, he jumped right on the bandwagon. He was a huge help and got so excited by the project that he did most of the work himself. I know I was very lucky, but most parent organizations would volunteer to help and some staff members might, too. In fact, my school parents were so thrilled with the hallway transformation, they volunteered to paint stripes in the cafeteria. It looked great!

THE CAFETERIA

This highly visible area should really provide a sense of students and school to all who enter. Encourage student displays of work. At the secondary level, invite homerooms or departments to create exhibits of student projects or bulletin boards with seasonal themes. These can become excellent advisory projects for individual homerooms. Have the school mascot and slogan painted on the wall. Decide upon a theme for the cafeteria and have a coordinated mural created. In the school my children attend, the students voted to have a jungle theme in their cafeteria. Over the summer, volunteer parents created a jungle mural. The students were thrilled with the results, and felt empowered by the opportunity to cast their vote for their favorite theme.

I firmly believe that student (K–12) artwork is not displayed enough in schools. The cafeteria can become an excellent place for ever-changing exhibits of this wonderful work. Laminate black poster-board frames and frame the work to give it a more professional look. Change the artwork weekly or biweekly. Perhaps student council members or office workers can make these changes when needed. Many schools have permanent student art displays, but short-term exhibits provide the opportunity for constant sharing of many different pieces throughout the school year.

Periodically provide table decorations. Whether they follow seasonal themes or are just a flower in a bud vase, this sets a more formal tone and students appreciate the added touch to their eating time. Some cafeterias have a "formal day" once a month, with tablecloths, flowers, and special napkins. Appropriate table manners are reviewed and everyone is to be on their best formal behavior this day. Many students are not aware of proper table manners, and this is an easy way to teach and reinforce this important societal skill at school.

Don't forget that most of these ideas are applicable to teacher eating areas. If the teachers don't eat in the cafeteria with the students, then make sure that the place they eat is comfortable and clean. Keep the room visually interesting and provide "creature comforts" whenever you can. Even though you probably won't have to have a "formal day" for teaching your staff table manners, some formal touches can make them feel special. Table-cloths, centerpieces, and a bowl of mints or chocolates can add a little panache to your lunch setting. Nice paper napkins are always appreciated, as is a special dessert now and then. Often your cooks will help you create these special treats, but you can also order sweets from a local bakery or deli. Some of you might even want to bake a homemade specialty!

CONFERENCE ROOMS

These are areas that deserve a bit of professional attention. Think about the events that occur in conference rooms (if you are lucky enough to even have one!): parent meetings, committee meetings, community resource meetings, and a place to bring visitors for coffee and conversations. This room should be a location where you and your staff can be proud to bring guests of the school. Make the room attractive and pleasant. Framed artwork, comfortable seating, plants, paper and pencil for note taking, a pitcher of water and glasses for refreshment all contribute to comfortable conferencing and meeting in this room.

Some schools also have a parent/teacher conference room. This room can be a bit less formal and house parent resources for checkout. A parent conference area can become a gathering place for visiting parents and a room where they can have parent board meetings or small committee meetings. This room can also be used for parent/teacher conferences or other special meetings between staff members and parents. Again, make this room welcoming with the same touches as above. Inspirational parenting posters can adorn the walls and rocking chairs can fill the odd corners. A conference room of this type could also become a Parent Welcoming Center. When new families arrive, you could spend some time here with them getting acquainted. Have folders of basic school information prepared; tuck in some school pencils, magnets, or notepads. Our student council made this a regular service project. They decorated the folders, placed the necessary materials inside, and presented the folder to the family upon arrival. Often they would give the student a tour of the building while I was meeting with the parents. This was always a positive way to begin a relationship with new families. Remember the basket of toys and books suggested for the principal's office section? This room is another good place to have a basket of goodies to keep young siblings playing contentedly.

Of course, one conference room can serve all purposes. In the school where I became principal, a small room housed a computer for management of a program unique to the school—and this was the room's sole use. I immediately saw multiple uses for the space. I went to my PTA board and shared my vision for this future conference room: a place for parent/teacher conferences, a resource center for parents to check out informational materials, a place for us to gather the visitors that came to our school, a place for teachers to have small-group meetings when needed, and a location for meetings of groups of students for various school clubs. I asked for $150 to transform the room. They felt my idea had merit and granted my request. I bought paint, wallpaper border, garage-sale furniture, lamps, fabric for curtains, and a few parent resources to get our collection started. With the donation of the time and talents of some teachers and my custodian, we had ourselves a great little conference room. After the first year of using the conference room, the PTA was so impressed with its many functions that they donated more money for additional resources.

CLASSROOMS

Allowing and encouraging teachers to apply these inviting principles to their classrooms can become a treat for everyone involved in the school. Teachers are so very creative and are masters at discovering endless possibilities for everything! After I took my staff to visit the school with a positive climate, they began such a wonderful transformation of their own classrooms. I watched more painting and stenciling than I could ever imagine. There were pale yellow walls with stenciled apples and light blue walls with stenciled dinosaurs. Plants, rocking chairs, lamps, curtains, beanbag chairs, aquariums, rugs, couches, and even lofts appeared throughout the building. Clutter and messy areas began to disappear. Student work was displayed more often, mobiles hung from the ceilings, and a student-made quilt was prepared for exhibit in the entrance hallway. The teachers and students worked very hard to make their classrooms feel more homey and inviting.

Teachers also learn where to go for the bargains that will help improve school climate. Many stores give away their seasonal posters and displays when they are finished with them. Don't be afraid to ask for these items. They might say no, but they more often say yes! While walking through a bookstore one day, I saw these wonderful posters with children reading on them. I asked about them and the manager said to come back in a couple of weeks to pick them up. After getting the posters, I laminated them and these posters adorned our hallways during National Library Week. I sent a thank-you note to the bookstore owner with a picture of the cheery hallways he had helped create with his donation. One teacher noticed that her child's daycare center was throwing out some colorful rugs. She asked for them and was loading the rugs in her van within minutes. We cleaned and vacuumed them, then they were placed in our kindergarten and first grade classrooms. One of my reading teachers found a vinyl couch at Salvation Army. She cleaned it up, added some throw pillows, and moved it into her classroom. I can still picture her on that couch, all nestled in, reading with her students.

Another simple climate element is music. Many teachers play soft music while students are working independently or during indoor recess time. Music can have a calming effect on all ages, from young children to adults, and provides an opportunity to introduce various styles of music to children. One of my favorites to hear in the classroom is classical music. Many children do not hear this music on a regular basis and the exposure is healthy for them. I will never forget watching a first grade classroom come in from recess. They were quite wound up as most first graders are after recess. The teacher had soft, classical music playing as they entered the room. You could just see their bodies relax and they began to speak quietly as they calmly began their next academic task. Music has a place in every classroom and can add an interesting ambiance to learning environments.

We can all picture wonderful classrooms where entering and staying is pure pleasure. Encourage and motivate your teachers to create these magical settings within your school. Compliment them when they have put effort into improving the appearance of their classrooms. The rewards go directly to the students, and the teachers have designed a room climate they find comfortable and inspiring to work in.

REMEMBER . . . IT BEGINS WITH YOU

You can become the catalyst for change in your building. Start with one or two small projects and model your vision and expectations in your office. You set the standard and the tone. If you can generate some interest, then go for it! Let teachers visit other classrooms and other schools. Some schools even have a climate committee devoted to continuously improving the look, feeling, and tone of the school. One principal shared that each spring and fall they have an all-school beautification day. Each classroom completes a project that will enhance the appearance of the school. Remember to consistently reinforce and encourage these efforts by recognizing them privately and publicly in your weekly staff memo.

I have also mentioned several times in this chapter the involvement of my custodians in this process. They can become key players in many of your endeavors. Make sure they are treated with the same respect, dignity, and professionalism you accord other faculty members. Their job can be just as demanding and difficult as anyone else's in the building. Let them know how much you appreciate them, and think of special ways to thank them for their efforts.

These changes can affect morale in numerous positive ways. Creating an environment people want to work in and feel comfortable in can only lead to greater productivity and job satisfaction. Happy teachers lead to happy students. Be conscious of the look and feel of your school. Model what you want and encourage creativity. You and your staff will create a school that you can be proud of both inside and out.

17

THE STUDENT-TEACHER LINK

Positive staff morale is essential for any school to be the best it can be. At the same time, the strategies that improve and encourage staff morale are the same concepts that can improve student morale. In addition, schools that have positive teacher morale also have a good chance of having students with high morale. The converse is also likely to be true. Examining this student-teacher link reveals more reasons to pursue strategies to improve morale.

TWO MORALES

Each school has at least two "morales." One is the morale of teachers and the other is the morale of students. It is essential that we understand how these two morales are interrelated. It is also critical to be aware that we can never sacrifice one for the other. Whichever of these morales is lowest will eventually bring the other down to its level. This is why it is essential to focus on enhancing both. Let's look at a couple of examples.

Suppose you decide to try to raise student morale by having soda machines available all day and allowing the students to take these beverages into any classrooms in the school. In the short term, the students will likely be quite excited by this and their morale will be given a boost. However, you can imagine what the teachers will feel about this idea. A few incidents of students coming late to class because the machine did not give them correct change, or spilling pop all over their homework papers, will quickly lower the morale of the teachers. As their moods become less positive, their attitudes will affect their students, gradually dragging student morale down to the same low level.

This relationship also works in the other direction. Suppose a principal, in response to teacher calls for more support in the area of discipline, decides that any student sent to the office will be suspended for 10 days no matter what the offense. The teachers, at least some of them, may feel a short-term boost in morale. "Finally, we are getting some support," may be the cry of a few. However, as students see the injustices that ensue, they will grow frustrated. They may not rebel directly, for fear of being suspended themselves, but gradually this simmering frustration will affect the staff. Initially, students may just be argumentative in class, in support of peers who are sent to the office for very minor offenses. Eventually, this concern may even lead to anonymous and threatening phone calls to staff members at home, or damage to cars in the parking lot. Teachers will also be more frustrated with each other. A student that most teachers have no trouble with in the classroom might be suspended for not bringing a pencil to another teacher's class. As you can see, teacher morale will gradually sink to the level of student dissatisfaction.

Recognizing and valuing the link between student and teacher morale is essential for an educational leader. Making sure that both are supported—that we do not sacrifice one for the other—is critical to maintaining the best possible staff disposition.

The focus of this book is on faculty and staff morale, but we do want to mention briefly the importance of student morale. Though what follows is not intended as a comprehensive examination of student morale, we thought it might be valuable to sprinkle in some quick reminders and ideas.

STUDENT SATISFACTION AND MORALE

Research has shown that many variables impact student morale. Two significant variables are school climate and effective leadership. These two factors have a direct impact on student achievement, student motivation, and student satisfaction with school.

This book has discussed many ways to increase staff morale. Utilizing these strategies is the first step to increasing student morale. Lumpa (1997) found that a strong predictor of student satisfaction in schools is the level of teacher satisfaction in schools. He also found that school climate and principal effectiveness were predictors of student satisfaction. This information shows the importance of school leaders and their direct effect on the morale of the entire school, including the students.

The student-teacher link, which in turn is directly linked to leadership, has been well documented through the years. Bulach, Lunenburg, and McCallon (1994) observed that a leadership style that enhances school climate also enhances student achievement. They note, "It is quite possible that principals who use a promoter style of leadership and involve students, parents, and community in the decision-making process may have higher achievement" (p. 17). A promoter style is described as being outgoing, enthusiastic, flexible, dominant, socially skilled, and people-oriented.

School climate has been identified as another important component of schools. In contrast with previous ideas that student achievement could be explained by family background or individual characteristics, Brookover, Beady, Flood, Schweiter, and Wisenbaker (1979) found that some schools in economically depressed areas were providing a quality education. They found that school climate accounted for a significant amount of student achievement. Bulach, Malone, and Castleman (1992) also found significant relationships between climate and achievement. Sutherland (1994, pp. 6–7) outlined several comments from teachers who thought their school was effective. One of the comments was "we really try to put the needs of our students first at our school." We, as school leaders, must always try to facilitate best practices backed by solid research. Staff and student morale is no exception.

Many studies have observed the direct relationship between effective schools and student satisfaction with school. Sabo (1995) stated that educators have recognized the desirability and importance of improving student attitudes towards schooling. Epstein and McPartland (1976) described the quality of life at school as a multidimensional construct with three basic dimensions: student satisfaction, student commitment to class work, and student reaction to teachers. Student satisfaction is defined as the general reaction that students have to school. Commitment to class work is the level of student interest in the educational opportunities offered to the students in their school. Student reaction refers to the students' sense of overall quality of the nature of student-teacher relationships.

Pintrich, Marx, and Boyle (1993) indicated three traditional behavioral indicators of motivation of an individual's behavior: choice of task, level of engagement or activity in the task, and willingness to persist at the task. Fulk and Montgomery-Grymes (1994) discussed what causes poor motivation in the classroom and practical strategies to maximize student motivation. They explained that student-perceived competence and student-perceived control are the two concepts that outline motivational difficulties. Students' perceptions of their competence is found to predict achievement more accurately than their actual ability. Perceived control suggests a strong relationship between students' perception of control and their achievement.

Fulk and Montgomery-Grymes (1994, p. 29) outlined a menu of techniques for motivating students:

1. Student involvement: This includes providing an assignment menu, allowing for flexible sequencing and due dates, incorporating self-scoring and self-correction, varying assignment length, and setting goals with the student.

2. Create and maintain interest: This includes providing each student with an optimal challenge, introducing lessons enthusiastically, varying presentation style, giving clear directions, setting clear expectations, and explaining relevance of the activity.

3. Affective variables: These include creating a positive environment, providing performance feedback, and recognizing achievement.

Hootstein (1994, pp. 32–34) suggested approaches to motivational strategies that focused on making learning relevant and interesting to students. The strategies evolved from reviewing the literature on student motivation and interviewing teachers and students. The following strategies focus on assisting students to understand the relevance of learning and on making learning more interesting:

1. Relate the learning task to the students' needs, interests, concerns, and experiences. Teachers may relate a task to the students' needs or those outside the classroom. Teachers also can make learning relevant by embedding students' interest in instruction, as well as by addressing students' strongly felt concerns.

2. Make explicit the intended value of learning. Students want to know what they will get out of the assignment, including the academic benefits they will receive.

3. Share and model the value of learning. Teachers should show enthusiasm when teaching. Teachers should also show that they value the process of learning and that they gain personal satisfaction from specific learning activities. In addition, teachers can share their interest in the subject matter.

4. Encourage students to pursue their own interest in active ways. Teachers can induce students to generate their own motivation to learn. Students need to be active as they experience many physical changes. As students pursue interests in active ways, they prefer socialization and working with their hands rather than just listening or reading (Hootstein 1993).

5. Stimulate curiosity by offering novel, surprising, and mysterious information. Any sudden change in a student's existence can stimulate curiosity.

6. Create a discrepancy by providing incongruous, conflicting, and paradoxical information. Teachers can gain a deeper sense of curiosity by offering students

something new and different from that which they already know. A moderate level of discrepancy arouses curiosity.

7. Ask thought-provoking questions and encourage students to ask their own questions. Teachers can create an attitude of inquiry to sustain attention by asking divergent questions designed to elicit opinions, generate predictions, and solve problems.

8. Make abstract content more concrete and familiar. In some cases, students may perceive the content to be abstract and remote from their experiences. Teachers can use examples, analogies, and stories to help students relate the material to their existing knowledge.

Lumsden (1994, p. 2) outlined ten strategies to promote the enjoyment of learning:

1. Actively involve students in the learning process;

2. relate content objectives to student experiences;

3. assess students' interests, hobbies, and extracurricular activities;

4. occasionally present information and argue positions contrary to student assumptions;

5. support instruction with humor, personal experiences, incidental information, and anecdotes that represent the human characteristics of the content;

6. use divergent questions and brainstorming activities;

7. vary instructional activities while maintaining curricular focus and structure;

8. support spontaneity when it reinforces student academic interest;

9. make a conscious attempt to monitor vocal delivery, gestures, body movement, eye contact, and facial expression to evaluate the degree of enthusiasm conveyed in one's teaching; and

10. review and redefine instructional objectives to determine if teachers value them and are committed to them.

Andrade and Hakim (1995, p. 66) suggested getting students to open up as a way to increase student satisfaction. They outlined the following:

1. On the first day of class, give students a questionnaire to complete, or invite them to write you a letter about themselves. The more a teacher can know about the students, the better equipped a teacher can be to build personal relationships with the kids.

2. Ask students who have not done homework or who have come in late to class to write a note explaining why. Students should see these notes not as a punishment, but as an opportunity to communicate privately with the teacher. This helps build trust.

3. Ask students to write learning logs. Logs are especially useful at the end of a class in which new material has been introduced.

4. Invite students to help solve classroom problems, such as lack of classroom participation by students or student interruptions.

FOCUS ON STUDENT NEEDS
(IMPROVING MORALE ONE STUDENT AT A TIME)

The idea of focusing on the needs of each and every student may seem overwhelming. We wonder how we can meet every need of every student. The reality is that we cannot. But this fact should in no way be an excuse not to try to do our best. If the students perceive that they are being respected and listened to, their morale shoots through the roof. When trying to improve student morale from a discipline perspective, I always try to put myself in the student's shoes. I ask myself two questions, "What motivated this student to get into this discipline situation?" and

"What can the student learn from this situation?" For example, while working as a middle school assistant principal, I was in charge of much of the discipline of that school. I saw students in my office for many reasons. I found that the students had several things in common with each other and with me, as well as with every human being in the world. They wanted to be respected, appreciated, and cared for. Because of this, I began to look at every discipline situation as an opportunity to address these three very basic human needs. Rather than the traditional "You know that fighting means three days in-school suspension," I started asking questions like "Did any of the younger kids that look to you for leadership see you fight?" This reminds the student that he is respected by his younger peers and that he is important. It also gives the student the opportunity to talk about the kids that might have been affected in a negative way by his fighting. The student sees that I recognize and care about how important he is. This also moves the conversation to a higher level than if I try to interrogate the student as "judge and jury." Sure, this boy still received three days in-school suspension. In no way am I advocating less discipline. As a matter of fact, I can have higher expectations because of this proactive approach. Hopefully this entire process will help the young man feel more appreciated, which in turn will help him internalize how important he is and can improve his morale.

Another way to increase morale one student at a time is to have older students work with younger ones. I started this procedure by accident. While working as an elementary principal, I was talking with Kevin, a fifth grade student, about his refusal to do his work in the classroom. This was well into the year and I knew Kevin was vying for the much-needed attention he was not getting at home. During our conversation, a first grade student was sent to my office for throwing rocks on the playground. At that point, I had to leave my office for a few minutes to visit with a parent. Instead of just having the boys sit there, I asked Kevin if he would talk to the first grade student about why throwing rocks was not a good thing to do. When I returned to the office, the two boys were having a great conversation about safety and what a great school this is. I saw Kevin was getting his much-needed attention from this first grade student. Kevin was being a mentor, which did more for him than for the young boy he was mentoring. From that day on, we developed a school-wide buddy system that allows all students to work with younger students throughout the building.

There are many ways school leaders can address this whole issue of increased student morale and pride at school. Providing opportunities for the fifth grade students to interact with the younger kids at a K–5 elementary is one example. Here are some other great ways to build student morale.

Talk to students about their special school. As principal, I enjoy getting together with each class at the beginning of the year and telling them how special they are and how they make our school a terrific place. This is in place of the traditional "go over the rules" speech. I ask them why this is a special place and what they can do to make it even better. I also let them know how they influence the other students. I do this by letting them know things like, "Every time you go to music you pass five rooms that hold 120 students," and "I am so proud to be a part of your school." This shows the students they are important and respected.

Tour other classrooms. Taking kids on tours of other classrooms gives them the opportunity to see other grades and to show their interest in each other. For example, you might take a sixth grade class into an eighth grade room and say, "Take a look at how every student is continuing to work while we are in here," or "Look at their work on the walls; if you do the best you can, you will be able to do this also." Conversely, you can take a fourth grade class into a first grade room and say, "Look at the future leaders of our school; look how great a job they are doing." Such visits expose students to other students, increase their respect for each other, and make good use of the enormous effect of positive peer relationships.

Offer "popcorn with the principal." This can be a Friday treat for "students of the week." At one elementary school, each teacher selects a student of the week. They can be chosen for any reason; the only rule is that every student gets this award at least once during the year. The students meet the principal in the cafeteria for half an hour on Friday afternoon. Popcorn and lemonade, purchased by the PTA, are served. The fifth grade can serve the younger students—yet another demonstration of their important leadership. Each student stands up and says his or her name, grade, and favorite thing about the school. The principal might give out certificates or surprises, lead cheers, or play games. The point is that kids of all ages get to know and respect each other, while celebrating their accomplishments.

Schedule cross-grade non-structured time. Have different grade levels and classes eat together. Schedule recess and free times with several grade levels. At the middle school level, this might mean different teams eating together. The objective is relaxed communication that builds morale and breaks down perceived barriers.

Celebrate, celebrate, celebrate. We, as people, need to celebrate our accomplishments. Students are no different. Some ways for a school to celebrate are having the whole school applaud for improved test scores, holding an all-night read-a-thon to celebrate spring, or announcing a high-five day—every time a student passes a teacher in the hall they give each other a high five to show respect for each other. Pick any reason you want, but be sure to celebrate. This is a terrific way to improve school morale.

Student morale goes hand in hand with staff morale. This chapter outlined research that shows this link, along with strategies to improve student morale. We, as educational leaders, are responsible for making every day the best experience possible for kids. Having great student morale is a key to accomplishing this. Improving morale brings increased satisfaction to everyone involved—and it is just plain fun.

PARTING THOUGHTS

If our goal has been accomplished, your mind is swimming with new ideas (or some old ones you had forgotten about) and your leadership has acquired additional spirit and purpose. Leading and inspiring people day in and day out is never an easy job. We hope that this book can become an inspirational and motivational tool that can continuously assist you as you work to make schools the very best place for all children.

William Butler Yeats once said, "Education is not the filling of a pail, but the lighting of a fire." Yes, this phrase rings true when we think about teachers educating children, but it also has a different twist for educational leaders. You must light the fire and the passion within the people you work with. They must be excited about their jobs and view your school—their school—as an invigorating place to practice their chosen profession. You have many tools to ignite these flames of enthusiasm. Don't forget that this is one of the most important aspects of the job you do each day. Your actions and decisions effect morale. When your teachers' morale is energized and productive, good things will happen in classrooms. When good things happen in a classroom, the future for every child in that room is brighter. Remember, that's why we lead schools. We lead so that our children can learn, grow, and succeed.

Your job is so vital to every breath a school takes. Make sure the air the school takes in is motivational and inspirational. If you succeed, your job will be a pleasure. Enjoy every minute!

REFERENCES

Adams, B., and Bailey, G.D. (1989). School is for teachers: Enhancing the school environment. *NASSP Bulletin, 73* (513), 44–48.

Andrade, A. M., and Hakim, D. (1995). Letting children take the lead in class. *Educational Leadership, 53*(1), 22–24.

Barth, R. S. (1990). *Improving schools from within.* San Francisco, CA: Jossey-Bass, Inc.

Barth, R. S. (1993). Coming to a vision. *Journal of Staff Development, 14*(1), 6–9.

Beck, A.C., and Hillmar, E.D. (1987). *Positive management practices.* San Francisco, CA: Jossey-Bass.

Berry, B., and Ginsberg, R. (1990). Creating lead teachers: From policy to implementarion. *Phi Delta Kappan, 71*, 616–621.

Bissell, B. (1992, July). The paradoxical leader. Paper presented at the Missouri Leadership Academy, Columbia, MO.

Blase, J., and Kirby, P. (1992). Bringing out the best in teachers: What effective principals do. Thousand Oaks, CA: Corwin Press.

Brookover, W., Beady, C., Flood, P., Schweiter, J., and Wisenbaker, J. (1979). *School systems and student achievement: Schools can make a difference.* New York: Praeger.

Bulach, C., Lunenburg, F. C., and McCallon, R. (1994). *The influence of the principal's leadership style on school climate and student achievement.* Speeches/conference papers. (ERIC Document Reproduction Service No. ED 374 506).

Bulach, C. R., Malone, B., and Castleman, C. (1992). *An investigation of the relationship of school climate to student achievement.* Paper presented at the annual meeting of the National Council of Professors of Educational Administration.

Burr, A. (1993, September). *Being an effective principal.* Paper presented at the regional satellite meeting of the Missouri Leadership Academy, Columbia, MO.

Campbell, D., Cignetti, P. B., Melenyzer, B., Nettles, D. H., Wyman Jr., R. M., (1997). *How to develop a professional portfolio.* Needham Heights, MA: Allyn & Bacon.

Curran, T.J. (1983). Characteristics of the effective school-a starting point for self-evaluation. *NASSP Bulletin, 67* (465), 71–73.

Covey, S. R. (1989). *The 7 habits of highly effective people.* New York: Simon & Schuster.

Darling-Hammond, L., and Berry, B. (1988). *The evolution of teacher policy* (Rep. No. JRE-01). Santa Monica, CA: RAND

Duke, D.L. (1989). What can principals do? Leadership functions and instructional effectiveness. *NASSP Bulletin, 66* (456), 1–12.

Epstein, J. L., and McPartland, J. M. (1976). The concept and measurement of the quality of school life. *American Educational Research Journal, 13*(1), 15–30.

Feigelson, S. (1998). *Energize your meetings with laughter.* Alexandria, VA: Association for Supervision and Curriculum Development.

Fulk, B. M., and Montgomery-Grymes, D. J. (1994). Strategies to improve student motivation. *Intervention in School and Clinic, 30*(1), 28–33.

Garten, T., and Valentine, J. (1989). Strategies for faculty involvement in effective schools. *NASSP Bulletin, 73*(515), 1–7.

Glatthorn, A. (1984). *Differentiated supervision.* Alexandria, VA: Association for Supervision and Curriculum Development.

Glatthorn, Allan A. (1994). *A quality curriculum.* Alexandria, VA: Association for Supervision and Curriculum Development.

Herzberg, F., Mausner, B., and Snyderman, B. (1993). *The motivation to work.* New Brunswick, NJ: Transaction.

Hootstein, E. W. (1994). Motivating middle school students to learn. *Middle School Journal, 25*(5), 31–34.

Howard, E., Howell, B., and Brainard, E. (1987). *Handbook for conducting school climate improvement projects*. Bloomington, In: The Phi Delta Kappa Educational Foundation.

Howes, N. J., and McCarthy, H. (1982). *Participative management: a practice for meeting the demands of the eighties. Paper presented at the Annual Meeting of the American Educational Research Association*. (New York, NY, March 19–23, 1982). (ERIC Document Reproduction Service No. ED 216 435).

Keefe, J., Kelley, E., and Miller, S. (1985). School climate: clear definitions and a model for a larger setting. *NASSP Bulletin*, 69 (484), 70–773.

Kelley, E. A. (1980). *Improving school climate*. Reston, VA: National Association of Secondary School Principals.

Kritek, W. J. (1986). *School culture and school improvement*. Reports -evaluative/feasibility. (ERIC Document Reproduction Services No. ED 277 783).

Lagana, J. F. (1989). Managing change and school improvement effectively. *NASSP Bulletin*, 73(518), 52–55.

Lumpa, D. K. (1997). *Correlates with teacher and student satisfaction in elementary and middle schools*. Unpublished doctoral dissertation, University of Missouri, Columbia.

Lumsden, L. S. (1994). Student motivation. *Research Roundup*, 10(3), 4 pp.

Lunenberg, F., and Ornstein, A. (1996). *Educational administration: Concepts and practices*. Belmont, CA: Wadsworth.

Maehr, M. L. and Ames. R. (1988). *Instructional leadership inventory*. Champaign, IL: MetriTech.

Martin, J. A., and McGee, M. L. (1990). *Quality circle/site-based management implementation in public school districts*. Reports – research/technical. (ERIC Document Reproduction Service No. Ed 327 984)

Maslow, A. (1970). *Motivation and personality*, rev. ed. New York: Harper & Row.

Mayo, E. (1933). *The human problems of an industrial civilization*. New York: Macmillan.

Moeser, E. L., and Golen, L. L. (1987). *Participative management: A labor management process that works for kids.* Reports – descriptive. (ERIC Document Reproduction Service No. ED 281 275)

Pellicer, L. O., Anderson, L. W., Keefe, J. W., Kelley, E. A., and McCleary, L. E. (1996). *High School Leaders and Their Schools, Volume II: Profiles of Effectiveness.* Reston, VA: National Association of Secondary School Principals.

Pintrich, P. R., Marx, R. W., and Boyle, R. A. (1993). Beyond cold conceptual change: The role of motivational beliefs and classroom contextual factors in the process of conceptual change. *Review of Educational Research, 63*(2), 167–199.

Sabo, D. J. (1995). Organizational climate of middle schools and the quality of student life. *Journal of Research and Development in Education, 28*(3), 150–159.

Stevens, M. (1990). School climate and staff development: keys to school reform. *NASSP Bulletin, 74* (529), pp. 66–70.

Stronge, J. H., and Jones, C. W. (1991). Middle school climate: The principal's role in influencing effectiveness. *Middle School Journal, 22* (5), 41–44.

Sutherland, F. (1994). *Teachers' perceptions of school climate.* Reports – research/technical. (ERIC Document Reproduction Service No. ED 379 214)

Tyler, R. W. (1989). The Role of the Principal in Promoting Student Learning. *Educational Planning, 7* (1), 38–42.

Whitaker, M. E. (1997). Principal leadership behaviors in school operations and change implementations in elementary schools in relation to climate. Doctoral dissertation, Indiana State University, Terre Haute, 1997.

Whitaker, T. (1999). *Dealing with difficult teachers.* Larchmont, New York: Eye on Education.

Whitaker, T. (1997). Three differences between "more effective" and "less effective" middle level principals. *Current Issues in Middle Level Education, 6*(2), p. 54–64.

Whitaker, T. (1995). Accomplishing change in schools: The importance of informal teacher leaders. *The Clearing House, 68*(6), 356–357.

Whitaker, T., and Valentine, J. (1993). How do you rate? How effective school leaders involve staff members. *Schools in the Middle, 3*(2), 21–24.

Whitaker, T. (1995). Informal teacher leadership—the key to successful change in the middle school. *NASSP Bulletin, 79*(567), 76–81.

Winter, J. S., and Sweeney, J. (1994). Improving school climate: Administrators are key. *NASSP Bulletin, 78* (564), pp. 65–69.